# Contents

First published in English in 1998 with permission of DG22, European Commission, Brussles

Copyright © 1998 Christiane Blondin, Michel Candelier, Peter Edelenbos, Richard Johnstone, Angelika Kubanek-German and Traute Taeschner

ISBN 1 902031 22 9

A catalogue record for this book is available from the British Library
Printed in Great Britain by Copyprint UK Ltd
Cover design: Charlie Tapper
Typesetting: Karin Erskine

Published by the Centre for Information on Language Teaching and Research,
20 Bedfordbury, Covent Garden, London WC2N 4LB

CILT Publications are available from: Grantham Book Services, Isaac Newton Way, Alma Park Industrial Estate, Grantham, Lincs NG31 8SD. Tel: 01476 541 000. Fax: 01476 541 061. Book trade representation (UK and Ireland): Broadcast Book Services, 24 De Montfort Road, London SW16 1LZ. Tel: 0181 677 5129.

# ■ PREFACE

Obtaining employment, drawing enrichment from the different cultures that constitute the uniqueness of our continent, meeting people beyond national frontiers, all of this presupposes that to the greatest extent possible the barriers of language between our citizens should be removed.

This is one of the principal objectives of the White Paper *Teaching and Learning: Towards the Learning Society:* to attain a situation in which everybody is able to acquire and maintain the ability to communicate in at least two community languages in addition to their first language. It is clear that this assumes a considerable degree of effort. That is why, in order to attain this aim within the most favourable conditions, it is desirable that a start on learning should be made at the pre-school level and that there should be a systematic follow-up during primary education. It has in fact been widely established that young children are particularly receptive to this form of learning.

An analysis of the evolution of early language teaching in the various Member States of the Union reveals a tendency that seems irreversible: children are learning languages at an increasingly younger age. It was in order to support this movement that the Ministers of Education of the Union adopted on 20 November 1997 a resolution on the early teaching of languages.

Most of the Member States have already gained valuable experience in this area. It was for this reason that the Commission decided to support the work of a group of researchers who had undertaken to analyse the outcomes of these experiences by examining what contributed to their success. This in fact depends on a conjunction of the efforts of a wide range of groups: policy-makers, teachers, parents… Without claiming to be exhaustive, the researchers' review illustrates a range of practices that took place and makes a number of very useful recommendations pertaining to these. In addition to establishing principles and practices for early language learning, the document indeed locates this within a broader perspective of general education.

A reflection of European identity and citizenship, plurilinguism is equally one of the essential elements of the society of knowledge that we are entering as we approach the end of the century. In order to face up to this major challenge, it is essential that we should know how to make the most of our opportunities. It is also from this perspective – and not in order to investigate children's performance in its own right – that major efforts should be undertaken in order to promote the early learning of languages.

*Edith Cresson*

# PRÉFACE

Obtenir un emploi, s'enrichir des différentes cultures qui font l'originalité de notre continent, aller à la rencontre des femmes et des hommes par-delà les frontières, tout cela suppose que soit levée, autant que possible, la barrière des langues entre nos concitoyens.

C'est l'un des objectifs majeurs que propose le Livre Blanc *Enseigner et apprendre, vers la société cognitive*: faire en sorte que chacun puisse acquérir et maintenir son aptitude à communiquer dans au moins deux langues communautaires autres que sa langue maternelle. Il est clair que cela suppose un effort important. C'est pourquoi, pour y parvenir dans les meilleures conditions, il est souhaitable de commencer cet apprentissage dès le niveau préscolaire et de la poursuivre de façon systématique pendant l'enseignement primaire. Il est en effet largement démontré que les très jeunes enfants sont particulièrement réceptifs à cet apprentissage.

Une analyse de l'évolution de cet enseignement dans les différents Etats membres de l'Union montre que se dessine une tendance qui semble désormais irréversible : les enfants apprennent les langues de plus en plus jeunes. C'est d'ailleurs pour appuyer ce mouvement que les Ministres de l'Education de l'Union ont adopté, le 20 novembre 1997, une résolution sur l'apprentissage précoce des langues.

La plupart des Etats membres dispose aujourd'hui d'une précieuse expérience en ce domaine. C'est pourquoi la Commission a souhaité apporter son aide aux quelques chercheurs qui avaient entrepris d'analyser les résultats de ces expériences en examinant ce qui fait leur succès. Celui-ci dépend en effet de la conjonction des efforts d'acteurs très divers: décideurs politiques, enseignants, parents... Sans prétendre à l'exhaustivité, ce document met en évidence un certain nombre de pratiques éprouvées et propose des recommandations très utiles pour un bon accompagnement de cette démarche. Au-delà des principes et des savoir-faire initiaux, il la place en effet dans la perspective plus large de l'éducation générale.

Facteur d'identité et de citoyenneté européennes, le plurilinguisme est également un des éléments essentiels de cette société de la connaissance dans laquelle nous entrons en cette fin de siècle. Pour relever ce défi majeur, il est indispensable que nous sachions mettre toutes les chances de notre côté. C'est également dans cette perspective – et non pour rechercher la performance elle-même – que des efforts importants doivent être accomplis pour la promotion de l'apprentissage précoce des langues.

*Edith Cresson*

# 1 INTRODUCTION

**INTENDED READERSHIP**

The present review is intended for those who hold posts of responsibility in relation to the policy, provision and practice of foreign languages at primary school or in pre-primary education. Inevitably it has implications also for education at secondary school. Its aim is to help clarify the sorts of choice that have to be made by policy-makers, education authorities, teachers and parents in a domain that has witnessed renewed expansion since the mid-1980s across member states of what was the European Community and is now the European Union.

**GENERAL CONTEXT**

In recent years, member states have gone through different stages of development in this domain, with some having behind them a fairly lengthy tradition, others attempting a second start after a frustrating initial experience in the 1960s and 1970s, and others making or contemplating their first major attempt. A great deal has been written on the subject, from which it has become clear that nothing seems to be definitively settled. This therefore seemed an appropriate point at which to attempt a review that would seek to establish a link between *the conditions* in which the various developments took place and *the results* that thus far have been attained. So far as the latter are concerned, to the extent that the aims that have generally been stated are not limited simply to outcomes for the learner but also envisage the construction of a linguistically pluralist Europe, it is appropriate to investigate any possible effects on the status of particular languages at school and, if possible, in society.

**SPECIFICATION OF THE DOMAIN**

The review is primarily concerned with foreign-language teaching that is restricted to a relatively small amount of time per week, even if this still allows for considerable diversity of activity. The focus of the review does not include bilingual education which we interpret as the use of a foreign or second language for teaching at least one other school subject, though within our text we do provide a small number of examples of bilingual education in order to show how different it is from our theme. The languages in question are essentially those commonly termed 'foreign', however adequate or inadequate this term may be on a continent in which the forces of history and of recent and current economic migration have often brought these languages to co-exist within one common political or administrative entity.

**A TOPIC THAT CURRENTLY GENERATES MANY QUESTIONS...**

The expansion of foreign-language teaching in pre-secondary education over the past ten years or so has not taken place in a uniform fashion across what is now the European Union. Many countries have reached the stage of small- to larger-scale experiments, often with an intention of subsequent full generalisation. In some cases, the generalisation has been achieved, or is on the point of being so. Moreover, the ages of the pupils in question may vary, all the more so since the number of years accorded to primary education is not the same across the different educational systems.

The objectives that have been pursued, the categories of teachers involved, the specific sorts of training available to them and the teaching approaches that have been recommended and that have in fact been applied constitute other important dimensions of a diversity on which some initiatives have already been able to draw, in order to capitalise on the wealth of experience that has been gathered and to promote exchanges of view that lead both to reflection and to action. This is particularly so in the case of the co-operative activities that have been put in place thanks to the support of the Lingua and Socrates programmes of the EC and also to Workshops 4A/B and 8A/B of the Council of Europe.

**...TO WHICH THUS FAR CLEAR ANSWERS HAVE NOT BEEN FOUND**

During the last few years a very large number of publications have been devoted to the teaching of foreign languages in pre-secondary education across the members states of the current European Union. Too often these only serve, in repetitious fashion, to make claims that have not in fact been grounded in genuine research or to describe situations that are too specific to permit any generalisation of conclusion.

**METHOD OF WORKING**

The review relies on selected empirical data obtained by relatively recent research that was considered by the team to be sufficiently rigorous. Care was taken to take account of the particular characteristics of the contexts in which the developments took place. A pluralist concept of research was maintained, with equal interest in those projects that focused mainly on learner outcomes and in those that mainly attempted to describe the processes that took place in the very act of learning or teaching. The criteria for selection of texts then were that they should be of sufficient quality, relatively recent, be based on empirical data, feature the normal provision of foreign languages in pre-school or primary education rather than bilingual or immersion models, deal with outcomes and with contextual factors relating to these, and occur within member states of the European Union. Most of the texts selected met these criteria, though a small number of other texts have also been briefly discussed that help to illustrate particular points.

In spite of considerable efforts to find suitable publications in the form of official reports, theses, articles etc. that met our minimal criteria, the number of texts that were assembled was not large. This seems all the more so when compared with the very much larger number of un-researched publications containing recommendations on aims, policy, methods and activities that have been devoted to this area. Indeed, our search proved a fascinating if somewhat daunting task. It was made all the more difficult, since there is at present no such thing as a community of European languages researchers that uses a common pool of journals through which to share with each other the fruits of their research. As a consequence, we had to read as widely as we could at the national as well as the international level, attempting to cover as many countries and languages as possible. We were able to benefit not only directly from the reports cited in our review and listed in the bibliography at the end, but also in a more general sense from several other studies that have been published on the topic but that were less empirical in nature. Despite our best attempts to access all relevant reports, we make no claim in these rather difficult circumstances to have identified a definitive set of research reports for the European Union as a whole. However, we do consider that in the time available we have been able to bring together a sufficiently substantial body of important research studies for us to be able to present key outcomes and contextual factors at a sufficient level of generality.

## AN INSTRUMENT FOR ANALYSING COLLECTED DATA...

In order to ensure that procedures for extracting data from the selected empirical studies were conducted in a rigorous manner and within a consistent conceptual frame of reference, the writing-group decided to devise a framework for analysis which is contained in the Appendix. The objective of this framework is to highlight both the conditions in which the developments took place and the results that were attained, plus any possible relationships that had been established between these two sorts of data. The framework was intended to enable a precise description to be made of the research design adopted for each study, so that the reliability and validity of the findings might be gauged and then taken into account within our overall review.

## ...AND ITS LIMITATIONS

Obviously the use of a framework does not permit the collection of the total amount of detailed information which may sometimes be found in the publications studied, particularly information pertaining to what occurs in any language course and that is acknowledged to have a determining influence on results. Nor is it ideally suited to the collection of data arising from small-scale qualitative research. Where research of this sort features in our review, it was not considered useful to apply the grid framework.

## USING THE FINDINGS

As has already been emphasised, particular care has been taken in our review in describing the social and educational contexts. It is our belief that there does not exist any 'good practice' as such nor any good solutions that are universally valid. There are, however, responses which appear, with more or less certainty, to be more or less sufficient to allow for the attainment of an intended outcome within a context that bears particular characteristics. It is from this perspective that data have been assembled and that this review is written. Each reader can and should use this review in accordance with their own objectives and within their own context.

**AIMS AND APPROACHES OF THE RESEARCH STUDIES**

Information was collected on research of different kinds that varied according to the specific aims of each study. Space does not permit a description of the particular research approach adopted for each particular research project. Broadly speaking, however, the following categories may be distinguished:

- *Comparing an experimental group that had been introduced to a foreign language at primary with a group that had not, on the basis of their performance on one or more common assessment tasks applied at some stage during secondary.* Here, the question could be: How did the experimental group perform in comparison with the other group? This approach tended to be adopted when the process of introducing a foreign language to primary schools in a particular member state was not complete, with the consequence that a comparison could be envisaged between those who had been introduced and those who had not.

- *Comparing the performance of pupils, not with that of a comparison group, but rather with agreed, pre-established national standards and criteria.* This pre-supposes that a national consensus had been reached concerning what pupils might reasonably be expected to achieve. Here, the question could be: 'How did the pupils perform in relation to what they were expected to be able to do?' 'Did they meet, or surpass, or fall below these pre-established standards?' This approach tended to be adopted when a state had more or less totally introduced the foreign language to all primary schools, so there was not much possibility of having a comparison group that had not had this experience. In this context, the opinions of experts such as experienced researchers or national inspectors might be required in order to reach a judgement as to whether a particular level of performance by pupils was or was not satisfactory. For example, if the level fell below expectations, would this imply the need for better teaching and resources or for more realistic national standards, or for both?

- *Comparing the performance of different groups of pupils following different conditions or approaches (to teaching) but within a population that had been introduced to a foreign language at primary school.* In such instances, the comparison might be between an experimental innovatory approach and a more conventional approach, in order to learn something about which approach was the more suitable.

- *Investigating processes of learning and teaching.* This fourth category does not directly address relationship between conditions and measured outcomes as such. Nonetheless, by offering valuable insight into processes that occur in the foreign language classroom during children's pre-primary and primary education, it helps us understand what their competence in their foreign language consists of and how it develops, and it offers us a suggestion of what can be achieved by children at this level involved in learning a foreign language. One example of research of this sort might be the investigation of children's processes of second-language acquisition during their learning of a foreign language in pre-primary or primary education. For example, what stages did children's lexical, grammatical and functional development appear to go through? Here, the research would not necessarily have to be of a macro-sort, based on fairly large samples of children. It might be a minutely detailed micro-investigation of a small number, intended not necessarily to reveal universal findings but to allow for the development of further hypotheses related to children's second-language acquisition within an institutional context. Where comparisons are made, these might not be with control-groups but rather with the existing research literature of the particular field. For example, did the findings tend to confirm or disconfirm or in some way add to these findings that had previously been published?

In the research reviewed, these four approaches were adopted, sometimes separately and sometimes in combination. It is already clear that the four approaches do not all address exactly the same sorts of question.

## DURATION AND SCALE OF RESEARCH PROJECTS

Most of the research discussed within our review has been published in the 1990s. As such it is fairly recent, though in a number of cases the actual conceptualisation of the research may have begun in the 1980s. What our review of course cannot embrace is the research that is currently taking place, as new researchers come into the field with in some cases new sorts of research question. For the most part we have limited our scope to research published within member states of the European Union, though in a small number of cases we have cited research from elsewhere, if it seems to have a particular relevance to our discussion.

The various research projects differed in duration and scale. Some were major national evaluation projects extending over a number of years, others were the initiatives of keen researchers working on a fairly small scale and with limited funds and staffing, while others were at points in between. In some cases the research was independent, while in others the project organisers also designed the research programme. For most research groups, it was not possible to apply a particular 'control-measure' or to cover a very large sample or to implement a particular research procedure to the extent that they would have wished, and at times they were ready to admit this in order properly to alert their readers to a limitation of their findings. In some cases these limitations have been mentioned in our discussion, but this is not necessarily intended as a criticism of the research. Where the term 'comparison' is used, this is not intended in a strictly scientific way, since in the domain of education it is rarely possible to control the complex range of interacting variables that are normally involved. What is meant here at best is a research design that will provide a useful comparison between an 'experimental' group of children learning a foreign language at primary and a different group that in some respects at least shares common characteristics.

## OBJECTS OF RESEARCH INVESTIGATION

If the different research projects differed in aims, approach, duration and scale, they differed also in what they were investigating. In some cases, they were investigating children beginning a foreign language late in their primary school career by means of limited exposure to the language; in other cases they were investigating the effects of input that came mainly from video-cassette rather than a trained teacher; in other cases they were investigating much younger children in early primary or pre-primary education; in other cases again they were investigating an approach based on 'awakening' children's interest in languages by introducing them to a number of these rather than on an 'initiation' in respect of one particular language.

**RAPIDLY CHANGING SITUATION**

In most member states the situation for languages at primary school can only be considered as one of rapid change and confusion. A few examples will suffice.

In France from the late 1980s a major initiative was implemented that introduced a foreign language to a large number of primary schools, with the teaching undertaken by a variety of teachers, not only the normal classteacher but also languages teachers from secondary and outsiders possessing competence in the particular foreign language but who had not necessarily been trained as teachers. Research discussed in the present review, e.g. Genelot (1996) pertains to the implementation of this initiative. It was decided, however, that this model of staffing was not a feasible basis for implementation across the entire country and so a new initiative was developed, whereby children from class CE1 (aged 7) onwards would receive fifteen minutes of a foreign language per day by means of video-cassette input with their usual primary school teacher. The video-material was prepared by a national team. Those many teachers who felt lacking in foreign-language competence would have this material available as the main source of language input for pupils. The first year of implementation of this substantially different approach was the object of a report by an expert team writing for the Ministry of Education (1996). In other words, the focus of research can vary considerably within national initiatives in the same country.

Another example of major change of direction at national level is to be found in Scotland, where the national pilot model of trained specialist secondary-school teachers of foreign languages visiting the primary schools in order to work alongside the primary-school teachers has now at the generalisation stage been replaced by a model in which the responsibility for foreign-language teaching at primary will rest almost exclusively with primary-school teachers.

In Germany, to offer one further example, there is a national consensus about the usefulness of primary-school foreign languages, but because of the educational and cultural autonomy of the different federal states, this was conceptualised in different ways, which understandably led to different types of research.

Within this picture of rapid change, one general factor should immediately be noted. Most if not all educational systems within the European Union have to survive in a climate of tough financial constraint. Inevitably, some initiatives on foreign languages at primary school will achieve their intended generalisation later than originally anticipated. These constraints will also affect the possibilities for further research in this important area.

In the following section, a number of key outcomes are presented. In some cases these are highlighted by a table (Figures 1–4) which draws attention to key outcomes and point towards key factors. Then there is a brief discussion of each of these key factors in turn. It proved impossible to adhere strictly to the initial intention of separating discussion of outcomes from discussion of the effects of contextual factors. In places, in the discussion of outcomes, it was judged helpful to make brief mention of particular contextual factors alongside these outcomes, but to do so in a way that would not pre-empt the more general discussion of contextual factors that would follow.

**SUMMARY**

Relatively few comparisons have been made recently at secondary school between the competence of pupils who were 'initiated' in a foreign language at primary and those who were not. Where such comparisons have been made, 'initiated' pupils who have had a longer period of instruction tend to show an advantage over 'secondary beginners'. This advantage may in some cases be limited to certain competences, e.g. listening comprehension, and to certain pupils, e.g. faster learners, and may not persist, though the longer-term effects through secondary have generally not been measured. In respect of metalinguistic competence, a few studies (all from similar contexts) show a positive effect on knowledge of how children's first language works.

A larger number of studies attempted to gauge outcomes at the end of or during pre-secondary education. In respect of communicative ability, the results are generally positive, even if in certain cases these are relatively modest and outcomes from comparison groups were not sought. Comprehension skills (listening and reading) seem to develop more quickly than skills in accurate, creative production. The learning of one foreign language at the pre-secondary phase was not shown to have a clearly positive impact on the development of children's metalinguistic competence. On the other hand, approaches based on a number of languages (not only foreign but possibly also first and second languages, dialects and minority languages) were found to have a positive influence on this. All the studies show very positive effects on the affective domain, with positive attitudes to languages, to culture, to speakers of the particular languages, to language-learning or to the development of self-confidence.

A small number of studies shed light on the relationship between the perceived status of particular languages and the choice of which language(s) to learn/teach in pre-secondary education. These suggest that the tendency to choose a major (dominating) international language is particularly strong in cases where one foreign language is to be learnt, and that quality of teaching can have a positive effect on diversity when offering a non-dominant language. At the same time, there is evidence to suggest that diversity can generate subsequent problems of organisation and continuity, unless the means necessary for supporting it are available.

**LONGER-TERM EFFECTS MEASURED AT SECONDARY SCHOOL**

## Communication in the foreign language

A small number of studies investigated the longer-term effects of introducing a foreign language at primary school, by taking one or more measures at secondary school. Generally, these measures were taken at a fairly early point at secondary school, so the truly longer-term effects have not been fully investigated.

Figure 1 summarises the key projects and findings, then in the ensuing paragraphs these are discussed. As a general principle, the order in which research projects appear in a particular Figure corresponds to the order in which they are discussed in the ensuing paragraphs. This order is not intended to be hierarchical. For convenience, in Figure 1 the letter E is used in order to denote Experimental pupils, i.e. those who studied a modern language at primary and were now at secondary, while C is used to denote a Comparison group of pupils who began their foreign language learning later, at secondary.

**Figure 1    Experimental and Comparison pupils: recent findings on foreign-language communication at secondary**

| Researchers | Date | Key features |
| --- | --- | --- |
| Edelenbos | 1990 | Advantage for E over C pupils maintained for three months at secondary but not after eight. Holland. |
| Kahl & Knebler | 1996 | E pupils superior to C in reading comprehension in early secondary, both in Gymnasium and 'orientation classes', though differences emerging within the E group. Hamburg. |
| Genelot | 1996 | E pupils after one year at secondary school showed slight advantage over C pupils in listening, reading and writing, but only in case of best pupils. Advantage disappeared after one further year. France. |
| Low, Duffield, Brown & Johnstone | 1993 | E pupils, after one year at secondary, showed advantage over two two cohorts of C pupils who had one and two years at secondary |
| Low, Brown, Johnstone & Pirrie | 1995 | respectively. Tentative signs that this advantage maintained to national examinations at age 16. Scotland. |
| Favard | 1992 1993 | Teachers perceived advantage for E pupils in habits of active listening, but no advantage in linguistic knowledge or performance. Based on inspection data. France. |

Edelenbos (1990) compared two groups of pupils in secondary education in Holland, the first having experienced two years of English at primary, with the other having begun English on entry to secondary. After three months at secondary, those who had experienced English at primary performed better, but this effect had disappeared after eight months, by which time both groups performed equally well. This study did not seek directly to measure pupils' attainments in the language but drew on teachers' own assessments of the general level of proficiency in English that their pupils had reached. Kahl & Knebler (1996) found that the experimental cohort (which had experienced English in Classes 3 and 4 of the primary school in Hamburg) were superior to the comparison group, when the attainments of both groups were assessed in Classes 5 and 6. In Class 5, where children had moved to an orientation stage (*'Orientierungsstufe'*) at early secondary in which primary methodology was maintained, the experimental children were superior to the comparison group when assessed for reading comprehension. In the case of children at grammar school, the superiority of the experimental over the comparison groups was maintained at the end of Class 6. Genelot (1996) indicated that after one year of secondary education the children who had been 'initiated' in a foreign language at primary school in France, in comparison with those ('non-initiated') who began at secondary, showed a slight advantage in respect of listening, reading comprehension and writing, but only in the case of the best pupils. However, this advantage had disappeared one year later. These findings applied to children both in heterogeneous classes (i.e. 'initiated' and 'non-initiated' pupils mixed) and in homogeneous classes ('initiated' pupils taught separately).

In their independent evaluation of the national pilot projects in Scotland, Low, Duffield, Brown and Johnstone (1993) compared the performance of 'project' pupils (who had experienced a foreign language for one or two years at primary) with two 'non-project' comparison groups. The 'project' cohort and one of the 'non-project' cohorts were near the end of the first year at secondary, while the other 'non-project' group was near the end of their second year at secondary. The 'project' cohort were found to be superior in respect of pronunciation / intonation, length of utterance and use of communication strategies, though there were no differences in grammatical control. This superiority was particularly apparent at the lower end of the achievement range. Subsequently it proved possible to track a sample of the first wave of 'project' pupils through to their first national examinations taken towards the end of fourth year at secondary (age 16). The performance in this examination of the particular schools (now with 'project' pupils for the first time at this stage) was compared with the performance of these same schools in previous years. The average results were the same as in previous years. However, in previous years only a minority of pupils had proceeded to take their first national examination in a foreign language (the majority having by that time opted out of the subject), whereas in the case of the 'project' pupils the great majority maintained their study and took the examination. The findings mean therefore that almost the full ability range of 'project' pupils had achieved the same average level of performance in the first national examination as the top 40% of the range in previous years.

On the basis of inspection visits to schools, Favard (1992, 1993) reported teachers at secondary (their perceptions rather than experimental findings) as tending to perceive some advantage for 'initiated' over 'non-initiated' pupils, but only in respect of having developed habits of active listening. No advantages were perceived in relation to linguistic knowledge or performance, these being considered to be 'uncertain, unequal and fragile'. When 'initiated' and 'non-initiated' children were in the same class, it was not possible to identify the 'initiated' children on the basis of their linguistic performance.

## Metalinguistic awareness

With regard to metalinguistic awareness, research in Italy (Pinto, 1993; Pinto, Taeschner and Titone, 1995) compared experimental and control groups aged 9–13 that were matched for age, socio-cultural family conditions, gender balance, district (various geographical contexts in Italy) and general intelligence. A special battery of tests of metalinguistic competence was developed in relation to children's first language. The experimental subjects, who had experienced a foreign language, proved to be more aware of the structure of their first language than were their control-group peers. The same research also indicated clear gains in early primary school (see later section).

## Cultural awareness

Genelot (1996) found that after one year at secondary those children who had been 'initiated' at primary school showed a slight advantage in respect of cultural awareness over those who had begun later, though this applied only to the most academically able pupils. This advantage was no longer observable one year later. The findings applied to 'initiated' children both in heterogeneous classes where they were mixed in with 'non-initiated' children and in homogeneous classes for 'initiated' children.

**MEASURED IN THE COURSE OF PRIMARY OR EARLIER EDUCATION**

### Communication in the foreign language

A larger number of studies investigated children's communication skills in a foreign language during or at the end of their primary education. Key aspects are set out in Figure 2 below.

**Figure 2    Recent research studies on the development of foreign-language skills at primary**

| Researchers | Date | Key features |
| --- | --- | --- |
| Edelenbos<br>Vinjé | 1990<br>1993 | Tests assessing national core goals in English for Grades 7 & 8 at end of primary. Performance in Listening and Reading judged satisfactory, room for improvement in Speaking. Holland. |
| Balke | 1990 | National assessment of children's English at end of primary. Performance in Listening judged satisfactory, Speaking less so. Sweden. |
| Ministry expert group, France | 1996 | Children at CE1 (aged 7–8) in first year of national initiative, mainly using daily 15-minute video-input. Results judged modest and below expectations. France. |
| Low, Brown, Johnstone & Pirrie | 1995 | Children aged 10 & 11 at primary, and 12 & 13 at secondary, all with experience of foreign language at primary, measured on same interactive task. Secondary pupils able to put more into the task, but 'more of same'. Little clear evidence of progression in creativity or range of expression or command of discourse. Scotland. |
| Peltzer-Karpf, Hasiba & Zangl | 1996 | Massive inter- and intra-individual differences in children's development of English grammar (morphology & syntax). All children seen to progress through same phases of foreign-language development from Classes 1–4. Lollipop programme (1 hour per week). Vienna. |
| Kahl & Knebler | 1996 | By end of year 2 of English (Grade 4), pupils had very large vocabulary, though spelling less secure. Hamburg. |
| Helfrich | 1995 | Teachers' judgements of children's ability and willingness to communicate at end of Grade 4. Over the years of the pilot, these judgements became more reserved. Rhineland-Palatinate. |

In Holland and Sweden the introduction of a foreign language in primary education has striking similarities: the language is English, it is an obligatory subject, specific goals have been formulated and empirical research has been undertaken to assess the level of proficiency of the children. The goals reflect the need for communicative competence supported by a positive attitude to foreign-language learning.

Communicative competence includes integrated skills in reading, speaking and listening within clearly-defined contexts. In the research by Edelenbos (1990) a test battery was developed for listening, reading, speaking, grammar and vocabulary (active and passive). Vinjé's (1993) project was part of the assessment of the level of education at the end of Dutch Primary Education (PPON), with tests assessing the 1987 core goals. Every five years the attainment level in English of over 2000 children within a nationally representative sample is measured. The learning outcomes after 30 contact hours in each of Grades 7 and 8 (children aged 10–12) were judged very satisfactory for listening and reading comprehension, though speaking required further improvement. These judgements (Vinjé, 1993) were based on a consultation of experts and confirmed by an independent evaluation by the inspectorate of education which indicated satisfactory results for English in primary education.

Balke (1990) reports on a Swedish national assessment of the attainment level of English at the end of primary education. The report reflects the major changes in the national curriculum for English occurring during the 1980s. The shift from grammatical to communicative teaching had been felt necessary, though this latter approach was not yet fully implemented. As a consequence, the results in tests of listening were average, though the results for speaking were not judged to be altogether satisfactory. It should be noted that the interpretation was based on comparing average results from one year to another, rather than on consultation with experts or on pre-established criteria.

In France, the interim report of the *Ministère de l'Education Nationale* (1996) on the 'initiation' of pupils in a foreign language during *Cours Elémentaire 1* (CE1) aged 7 to 8 years, found that the results were modest and below what had been anticipated. The main source of language input was a daily 15-minute lesson based on nationally produced video-cassettes, with the teacher generally playing a facilitative role rather than being the primary source of foreign-language input and interaction. Children experienced great difficulty in separating out the different elements in language formulae that had been learnt globally and in recognising language forms that were similar to each other. They enjoyed repeating what they had learnt, and when they did this immediately after hearing phrases on the video-cassette these repetitions were generally accurate. Their pronunciation did not always reflect possible errors made by their teachers but was often confused, unstable and removed from an authentic model. Creativity in oral expression was seldom evident, and children's utterances tended to be variable and atomised, with each new aspect of skill acquired tending to banish rather than enhance what had preceded it. On the other hand, children had more success in performing songs accompanied by meaningful gestures and in expressing utterances that were linked to activities characterised by discovery and playful competition.

The second phase of the independent evaluation in Scotland (Low, Brown, Johnstone and Pirrie, 1995) focused more on progression within the 'project' cohort rather than on the comparison of 'project v non-project' that had characterised the first stage of the research. It was not possible to follow the same pupils from one year to another (i.e. longitudinally) but a comparison was made at the one point in time (i.e. cross-sectionally) of children in Primary 6 (aged 10), Primary 7, Secondary 1 and Secondary 2 (aged 13), all experiencing or having experienced a foreign language at primary. All four year-groups undertook the same 15-minute paired-speaking task with a researcher. The intention was to establish whether the children at Secondary 1 and 2 would be able to put a richer mixture of language into the task than the children still at primary. Detailed analysis of the children's utterances was undertaken based on transcriptions of the audio-recordings. It was found that the children at Secondary 1 and 2 were able to put more language into the paired interview but this tended to be 'more of the same' rather than a richer mixture. There was little progression, for example, in range of verbs and adjectives and little development of children's ability to manipulate language at the level of sentence or discourse. The children's colourful, active and memorable experiences at primary school had helped some of them to assemble large chunks of language which they could pull out of their long-term memory store and produce with some fluency and confidence, but this had not yet led to an ability to manipulate structure in spontaneous speech, though there was some initial evidence of this in their writing. In seeking to explain these phenomena, the research team pointed both to a manifest lack of continuity between the children's experiences at primary and secondary levels, with a tendency for teachers at secondary to fail to build adequately on what children had begun to develop at primary, and also to a lack of metalinguistic emphasis in the teaching at primary.

In a study of Austrian children in the 'Lollipop' programme (one hour of English per week) the evolution of foreign/second-languagecompetence was observed from Grades 1–4. With regard to vocabulary, for example, Peltzer-Karpf, Hasiba & Zangl (1996), found a preference for adjectives over other sorts of word, though these tended to be limited to adjectives of size, extension, surface, structure and weight. The children could form positive and negative expressions and had a capacity for linguistic invention, e.g. *'applebaum'* (hybrid composition). Their morpho-syntactical development was characterised by massive inter- and intra-individual differences, though all the children showed similar patterns of syntax acquisition: In Class 1 they were able to produce mini-dialogues with essentially 1-word utterances and made much use of non-verbal strategies; in Class 2 there were fewer non-verbal acts and an increase in the use of formulaic chunks; in Class 3 there were more mistakes, a sign that spontaneous rule-creation had begun, and connectors such as *'when'* and *'because'* were being used. In another study of children on the Lollipop project, Seebauer (1996) found that some mistakes in pronunciation seemed to be developmental and not related to foreign-language acquisition, in that British comparison groups made the same mistakes. Kahl and Knebler (op cit.) showed that the children in Hamburg when performing spontaneously showed confusion between *'is'* and *'are'* and incomplete sentences such as *'the boy eating'*, while also in Germany (Rhineland-Palatinate) Helfrich (1995) found that although teachers formed positive judgements of their pupils' ability and willingness to communicate after two years by the end of Grade 4, these judgements gradually became more reserved. This however does not necessarily mean that children's rate of progress was declining; it may simply have signified a more realistic understanding of what was happening, as an initially enthusiastic view (possibly the 'Hawthorne effect') began to wear off.

Finally in this sub-section, we considered it appropriate to mention two studies featuring bilingual (partial immersion) approaches, in order to provide a contrast with the more limited situation that features in most studies of the present review.

The research on the Vienna Bilingual School (Peltzer-Karpf, Dringel-Techt, Jantscher & Zangl, 1996; Peltzer-Karpf & Neumann, 1996) drew on the same methodology as the research on the Lollipop programme and gave special insight into differences between conventional and more intensive approaches. The team observed L1 German, L1 English and multilingual children. Only some of the central results are summarised here. In the field of morphology, cognitively simple and perceptually salient patterns were recognised and acquired earlier than those that were less simple and salient, even at intermediate levels of competence. By Class 4 children possessed a good basic knowledge of rules and a capacity to analyse new language material. A basic morphological knowledge was observed even among those children who has the least favourable starting conditions. It was shown that syntax develops in an evolutionary process, with 'old' rule systems co-existing for a while alongside 'newer' ones before being replaced by them. This is how regression in Class 3, which was observed among some children, may be accounted for. According to the researchers, the two decisive factors contributing to the success of the children were: high-quality, finely tuned input due to the presence of native-speaker teachers and the peer-group effect, with L1 English children as communication partners. Nonetheless, even after four years of intensive contact, the research confirms that L1 German children cannot be expected to have turned into full bilinguals.

The on-going research in Berlin (Doyé, 1997), undertaken at the *Staatliche Europaschule* which has over 1500 pupils in reciprocal immersion classes in several language combinations (German plus Russian, French, English, Spanish, Italian, Greek or Turkish) first concentrated on listening comprehension. Three trends have emerged thus far in the first tests of listening comprehension in the German/English, German/French and German/Russian classes. (The children were tested for comprehension in their respective partner language.) First, the performance of the L1 English, L1 French and L1 Russian children in German surpassed, on the average, the German children's performance in the partner language. Most likely it is the factor of exposure which is responsible for this. Second, performance within the six tested language-combination groups varied from site to site (to explain, some language combinations were larger, so the 300 German/English children, for example, were spread across several sites in Berlin) and from class to class. Third, a comparison of all classes irrespective of the language group and site factor showed significant differences. The performance of some classes of different language groups and sites proved to be more similar than the performance of classes of the same language groups and sites. The reasons for these results have not been fully analysed.

## Development of metalinguistic aptitudes

In this sub-section the focus is mainly on metalinguistic aspects, i.e. the acquisition by children of what in English now tends to be called 'knowledge about language' (KAL) and 'language awareness'. This entails the awakening (hence the term *éveil* in French) in children of insights into, interest in and curiosity about language. The teacher may discuss with them what language is as a fundamental and distinguishing characteristic of the human species, what the component parts of its underlying structure are, how languages are learnt and used, how one language differs from another, how a local or regional language relates to the standard or the national language of a particular country, which mother tongues are represented in the school. An approach based on *éveil* can be very different from one based on *initiation* to one particular foreign where the aim tends to be language-learning rather than language awareness.

The meaning of the term may be extended beyond knowledge or awareness of language and be applied to awareness of strategies for language-learning or language-use. Metalinguistic knowledge then may be viewed as an important ingredient in learning a particular foreign language, or it may equally be viewed as an educationally valuable acquisition in its own right, perhaps affording children a wider experience of languages so that they may make their own more autonomous choice of which foreign languages they would subsequently wish to learn.

Figure 3 overleaf sets out some key findings in relation to children's development of metalinguistic awareness.

**Figure 3      Development of metalinguistic awareness (MLA) in children at primary**

| Researchers | Dates | Key features |
|---|---|---|
| Luc<br>Bailly et Luc | 1992<br>1992 | Children learning two foreign languages in Year 5 at primary on an approach with strong MLA element. Positive gains in MLA. France. |
| Charmeux | 1992 | Children in Years 2–5 at primary introduced to 7 languages and aspects of standard-regional varieties of French as language of school. Gains made in MLA. France. |
| Nagy | 1996 | Children in Year 4 at primary, with varying ethnic and linguistic backgrounds, introduced to various languages. Gains in MLA. France. |
| Favard | 1993 | Children learning one foreign language at primary. Assumption of slight but not clear gains in MLA, e.g. sound discrimination. Based on school inspection. France. |
| Genelot | 1996 | Children learning one foreign language at primary achieved lower level of MLA for French as L1 (or school language) than children not receiving foreign language at primary. France. |
| Pinto | 1993 | Children aged 4-6 on an approach incorporating a foreign language and their first language (standard and dialect) developed greater metalinguistic awareness of first language than comparison group children educated through first language (standard) only. See also Pinto for children aged 9–12. Italy, various areas. |
| Low, Duffield, Brown, Johnstone<br>Low, Brown, Johnstone, Pirrie | 1993<br><br>1993 | Children learning one foreign language. 11-year-olds had developed more awareness of language-learning strategies than 8-year-olds, including strategies for anxiety-handling and planning. Little evidence of emergence of MLA in relation to knowledge about language. |

First a number of studies focusing on metalinguistic knowledge are reported that derive from an approach based on *éveil* (awakening) to a number of languages. Then there is discussion of the extent to which approaches based on *initiation* (to one particular language) in fact appear to succeed or to fail in enabling children to develop this valuable ingredient.

A number of studies in France reveal a strong interest in *'éveil'*. Luc (1992) and Bailly & Luc (1992), in their research for the *Institut National de Recherche Pédagogique* (INRP), found that children who had simultaneously learnt two foreign languages in the fifth year of primary education by means of an approach in which metalinguistic awareness played an important role, developed an interest in how language works and in differences between languages. In an investigation of children in the second to fifth year of primary education, based on an 'awakening' approach to seven languages and on standard-regional language bilingualism, Charmeux (1992) tentatively concluded, though accepting that this was without being able to adopt strict evaluative procedures, that this approach had had a positive effect on the development of children's metalinguistic and metacommunicative abilities. The children proved to be capable of constructing for themselves notions about language that would previously have been considered difficult, had developed positive attitudes and skills in reading, and took pleasure in written expression and translation. Nagy (1996) investigated an *'éveil'* approach in respect of children in fourth year of primary education, featuring a number of different languages. On the basis of audio-recordings of classroom processes, the author concluded that 'contrairement aux idées reçues, peu de sujets sont trop ardus pour les enfants de cet âge' (Nagy, 1996: 276) (Contrary to received ideas on this matter, there are few subjects that are too demanding for children of this age). Eight months afterwards, a questionnaire and a discussion with the children revealed that they had no difficulty in remembering, sometimes in minute detail, the themes of the activities and the nature of the tasks in which they had engaged.

Positive outcomes in respect of metalinguistic awareness arising from *'initiation'* rather than *'éveil'* were less evident in France. Favard (1993: 8) reported that children who had received 'initiation' were more able than their non-initiated counterparts 'de discriminer des sons, des schémas prosodiques... de comprendre globalement un langage sonore ou de rechercher des informations ciblées' (in sound discrimination and in understanding sequences of sound globally or obtaining information that was being sought). It was reported, though not on the basis of test results or statistical comparison, that this advantage persisted for at least a year and that 'initiated' children maintained a stronger motivation than 'non-initiated' children that also lasted for a year at least. Genelot (1996), on the other hand, found that children who had been 'initiated' in one foreign language at primary school showed a level of metalinguistic competence in French as first language that was lower than that of those classmates of theirs who had not received this initiation. The longer the period of 'initiation' had lasted, the less positive the results were in this respect. It should be noted that this also applied to linguistic abilities in French, i.e. in use of the mother tongue. The findings on this were gathered by comparing the achievements of children taking nationwide assessments.

In various parts of Italy (Pinto, 1993; Pinto, Taeschner and Titone, 1995) studies have been conducted into the effects of foreign-language learning on pupils aged 4-6 years. The experimental group received a foreign language plus Italian, both in standard and regional variety forms, whereas the comparison group were educated through standard Italian alone. The two groups were matched for age, socio-cultural background, gender, location of home and general intelligence. The findings, based on specially devised tests of metalinguistic awareness, showed that the experimental group had acquired a deeper awareness of the structure of Italian than the comparison group. The evaluation research in Scotland (Low *et al*, 1993; 1995) found that many teachers suspected that pupils' learning of a foreign language at primary had helped them somewhat with their first language, though they did not articulate the precise ways in which this had come about. One sub-study within the research made a preliminary investigation of pupils' perceptions of learning strategy. In this, 8-year-old beginners were compared with 11-year-olds who had been learning a foreign language for two years in the same schools. The 11-year-olds were different from the younger children in that (a) they revealed a number of strategies for dealing with 'language anxiety', whereas the 8-year-olds revealed none, and (b) their thinking was directed to the future as well as to the present, whereas the younger children seemed more locked into the immediate present. The researchers concluded that the 11-years-olds were beginning to become somewhat 'language anxious', which was understandable in view of their imminent transfer to secondary. It was considered commendable that they were developing strategies for dealing with this.

## Attitudes, self-confidence, curiosity, interest

The above research projects also highlighted a number of other aspects of language-learning and use, such as attitudes, self-confidence, curiosity and interest, that may be considered to be associated with, though different from, the development of metalinguistic knowledge. The findings are summarised in Figure 4.

**Figure 4    Development of attitudes, self-confidence, curiosity and interest among children learning a foreign language at primary**

| Researchers | Dates | Key features |
|---|---|---|
| Edelenbos Vinjé | 1990/93, 1993 | Children developed very positive attitudes to learning English by end of primary education, though not yet fully confident. Holland. |
| Low *et al* | 1993/95 | Children learning a foreign language at primary were more confident than those beginning at secondary; also they were more willing to use risk-taking strategies and to initiate in talk. Scotland. |
| Mitchell, Martin & Grenfell | 1992 | Children on 'caroussel' approach to three foreign languages developed positive attitudes, less so in respect of intercultural understanding. England. |
| De Leeuw | 1995, 1997 | Children can be helped to become aware of their unconscious learning strategies. This enables them to assume greater ownership of their learning and thereby improve. Germany. |
| Pelz & Bauer | 1990 | French and German children interacting in 'encounter' groups tended to differ in their use of communication strategies, and some contexts were more successful than others in eliciting real language. Germany, France. |
| Nagy | 1996 | *Eveil* approach helped develop children's self-confidence towards learning and using another language, their enthusiasm, curiosity and tolerance of non-standard accents. Particularly helpful for children from minority language groups. |
| Charmeux | 1992 | *Eveil* approach served to develop children's confidence in their linguistic potential, their curiosity, interest and openness. France. |
| Luc | 1992 | Children who learnt to verbalise their hypotheses about the foreign language developed self-confidence. France. |
| Haenisch & Thürmann | 1995 | Learning a foreign language stimulated children's curiosity about language (but there was little effect on development of their first language). Germany. |
| Petillon | 1995 | Children tended to perceive learning a foreign language as difficult but this did not prevent them from rating it as their second-favourite subject at primary. Germany. |
| Gompf | 1996 | Games, songs and creative approach regarded favourably by children. Germany. |

*continued*

**Figure 4    Continued**

| Researchers | Dates | Key features |
| --- | --- | --- |
| Andreas | 1996 | Children's attitudes to learning a foreign language at primary gradually improved, though there was much variability and instability. Germany. |
| Gangl | 1997 | An interactive approach to teaching the foreign language helped children develop open attitudes towards the culture. Austria. |
| Sandfuchs | 1995/96 | Contact between children from Italian and German-speaking groups within same primary school project gradually led to less inter-cultural |
| Riccò | 1996 | conflict and to viewing the other group as normal. Germany. |
| Helfrich | 1995 | Teachers' judgements of children's ability and willingness to communicate at end of Grade 4. Over the years of the pilot, these judgements became more reserved but the initiative did not create negative attitudes. Germany, Rhineland-Palatinate. |
| Djigunovich | 1995 | Children in first and third year of primary, learning English, had positive attitudes but the nature of the attitude had evolved. from feeling positive about the pleasurable classroom activities to feeling positive about learning a foreign language. Croatia. |

In Holland, a number of studies (Edelenbos, 1990 and 1993; Vinjé, 1993) found strong evidence of very positive attitudes among pupils at the end of their primary education towards learning English, despite the fact that they were less than completely confident in using the language in complex communicative situations. This may be explained by the fact that much of their teaching is geared to using the language in structured contexts. The pupils' positive attitudes were also maintained despite the fact that the attitude of teachers in primary schools (e.g. Edelenbos & Hulsman, 1987) was not always as positive. In Holland, however, no long-term studies of children's attitudinal development in relation to English at primary school have been reported.

The Scottish research (Low *et al,* op cit.) found the children who had experienced a foreign language at primary to be more confident than those who had not. For example, they were willing to make use of risk-taking strategies, such as making words up even if these did not exist, during a paired interview with an adult researcher, and they were more willing to initiate utterances in classroom lessons. Mitchell, Martin & Grenfell (1992) report on children in the south of England in which the local authority employed foreign language assistants (French, German, Spanish) to introduce children at primary school to these three foreign languages on a 'caroussel' basis: one language for a while, followed by another and then another over the period of a year. The approach aimed to raise awareness of language and culture. The evaluation revealed positive attitudes on the part of the children but little evidence of gains in intercultural understanding. This suggests that in certain school contexts incidental learning of something as subtle as culture will not necessarily occur. If an aim is considered to be important, then teachers may require preparation for it in order to focus their teaching appropriately.

In Germany, De Leeuw (1995, 1997) showed that children can be helped to become aware of their unconscious learning strategies. He concludes that this enables them to take more ownership for their learning and thus improve. De Leeuw also addressed the anxiety factor which tended to be neglected or played down because of the enthusiasm that prevailed in the early 1990s. He showed that children were aware of their anxieties and that they developed different strategies for coping with them. The bi-national initiative featuring French and German on both sides of the Rhine, launched in 1984, offers the unique possibility of observing real encounters between peers of the respective languages because of the regular contacts (several times per year) that characterise the initiative entitled *Learn your neighbour's language* based on three hours per week voluntary participation from Grade 3 in Germany and CM1 in France. The researchers (Pelz & Bauer, 1990) found that a typical encounter embraced twenty-two situations (greetings, game, walks etc.). They also analysed the language functions that were used (their type and frequency), limiting themselves to the communication that took place in French. The German children made little use of communication strategies such as translating, paraphrasing, signalling incomprehension. An additional trend to be noted was the increase of 'real' communication, e.g. during meals and games. The language functions in French used most often were 'contact-making' (in class 20% of the total number of functions; out of class 8%) and 'requesting' (in class 13%; out of class 20%). Very few utterances were expressions of feeling.

These studies from Germany and Scotland form part of a rapidly expanding body of research on learners' foreign-language learning strategies. Most of this research has been applied to adults and adolescents, and so much remains to be learnt about the strategies that pupils adopt when at primary school.

Nagy's (op cit.) research suggested that when twenty-five children on an *'éveil'* approach were compared with a similar number of other children, more children in the *'éveil'* than in the other group possessed sufficient self-confidence to envisage that they could learn some useful words and expressions if they had to go to a foreign country. The *'éveil'* group indicated a preference for speaking the language, whereas the other group would rely more on gestures. They also showed more evidence of enthusiasm for and curiosity about language. Among the children who were subjects of this particular research, a number were speakers of one or more ethnic minority languages. These children showed considerable pride when they saw their language as the central focus of attention in class. On the same approach, the children who were not speakers of an ethnic minority language showed that they did not discriminate negatively between languages. In response to an item in the questionnaire on whether or not the children found certain languages ugly, the *'éveil'* group were more numerous in considering that an accent was normal and worthy of respect. The author, while accepting that there was a certain weakness in the size of sample and an absence of strict procedures of comparison, surmises that the approach had helped the children to discuss profitably questions of identity and inter-ethnic relations. Charmeux's (op cit.) research likewise pointed to considerable confidence among the children in their linguistic potential. There was also evidence of curiosity about language, an interest in languages and an open attitude towards pronunciation and different accents and varieties of French. The INRP research (Luc, 1992: 81) found that 'le fait de verbaliser son hypothèse et d'en solliciter la confirmation constitue un puissant facteur de sécurisation' (the fact of being able to verbalise one's own hypothesis and to solicit confirmation about this helped children to build up their self-confidence). It also found, on the basis of audio-recordings in class, that the children concerned had developed an open and questioning attitude to languages.

In the NorthRhine-Westphalian project, 90% of the teachers (Haenisch & Thürmann, 1995) believed that the children's curiosity about languages had been kindled, though there was little noticeable effect on mother-tongue teaching. A study by Petillon (1995) in the Rhineland-Palatinate, drawing on the self-assessment of 184 pupils, focused on the notion of difficulty as perceived by the children. Their foreign language was ranked fourth (with both mathematics and their first language ranked as more difficult). In response to an item pertaining to their favourite subjects, the foreign language was ranked second, after physical education. This suggests that the children were very positive about their foreign-language learning, even though they realised it was not always easy. In an interview study of 883 children, Gompf (1996) found that an approach which used games, songs, arts and crafts, and which allowed children to find 'English' material in their surroundings, was regarded favourably by the children. 79% of the children were not found to be motivated by the thought of obtaining good grades, and the weaker learners with low marks in German (first language or language of the school) were strongly opposed to this idea.

A number of studies in Germany and Austria investigated children's attitudes towards culture. In the Bavarian research (Andreas, 1996) children were asked in a pre-test 'What do you know about…?' Most associations with Austria were about nature, with food for Italy and tourist sights for France and England. In 1992 there were no differences between the experimental and comparison groups. Answers improved with subsequent experimental cohorts because the teachers had introduced more geographical aspects into their teaching. In a sentence-completion test designed to reveal children's attitudes, the responses indicated considerable variability and instability. This was explained as having two main reasons: first, little systematic teaching of culture had taken place; and second, the results were based on teachers' judgements arising from personal experience rather than on measurements. Andreas cautiously concludes that the mere fact of learning another language may lead pupils to form more reserved judgements, e.g. 'They are like us; some are nice, others are stupid.' Gangl's (1997) research in Austria showed that with a co-operative, interactive approach it was possible to open children up to other cultures, this being established on the basis of interviews with the participating children who indicated they would like to go to England and have English pen-pals. Riccò's (1996) report on the Wolfsburg project, which is based on intense contact between children from two different language groups, showed that children slowly learnt to experience each other as normal and not to identify each other primarily through their linguistic or national characteristics. Intercultural team management between the German and Italian teachers proved to be crucial, and some children experienced a phase in which they were reluctant to participate in Italian lessons, but this was gradually overcome. The research in NorthRhine-Westphalia (Haenisch & Thürmann, op cit.) reported that 70% of the teachers believed the project had enhanced children's willingness to become more open to other cultures. Helfrich (1995) studied children in the Rhineland-Palatinate, in respect of teachers' perceptions of pupils' attitudes towards foreign culture. From the teachers' responses the researchers concluded that the initiative did not create negative attitudes. However, over the four years of the pilot study teachers' responses became somewhat less enthusiastic.

Although care has been taken in the present review to limit the scope to research within members states of the EU, it was considered helpful to include mention of one particular study in Croatia, dealing with the development of children's attitudes to foreign-language learning. In Classes 1 and 2 at primary in the pilot projects centred round Zagreb, children receive one hour per day of a foreign language, which reduces to 45 minutes per day thereafter, from teachers possessing a competent command of the language (English, French, German or Italian) and with very impressive results achieved in relation to pupils' foreign-language development. Djigunovich (1995) reports that the same children were interviewed during their first and third years of foreign-language learning at primary, i.e. aged six and eight. Among the aspects probed were children's attitudes to the foreign language, native speakers, the purposes of foreign-language learning, the optimal age to start, foreign-language lessons at school and pupils' attainments. Analysis of the interviews revealed a subtle yet important process of attitude-development. Whereas the children aged six enjoyed their foreign-language activities because they were 'fun', by the age of eight these same children were now taking pleasure in activities because they were geared to 'language-learning'. The approach that their teachers had adopted, in which metalinguistic awareness arising from regular classroom discussion about their first language was seen as central, had enabled the pupils to become aware of a special process called 'language-learning' and were deriving pleasure from undertaking classroom activities that promoted this.

## Perceived language status and language choice

Our chapter on 'outcomes' concludes with a discussion of the perceptions of parents and of teachers in respect of the status of particular languages and the choices that are available to them. In presenting these two notions of 'language status' and 'language choice' as outcomes, we are suggesting that parents' and teachers' perceptions are influenced by the contextual factors that we shall be discussing in the ensuing chapter. We shall be arguing that they arise, to some extent at least, from decisions taken within the educational system on whether to teach children one foreign language at primary or to introduce them to a variety.

The NorthRhine-Westphalian study (Haenisch & Thürmann, 1995) showed that if the option of which foreign language to choose is left to the school, 74% opted for English, which may be interpreted as one quarter of schools being willing to take a risk with a 'smaller' language. French was chosen by 11%, meaning that 15% remained as an indicator of interest in plurilingualism. In this case, a perception among parents and pupils within one particular society of the major importance of English, combined with an educational decision to expose children to one foreign language, led to English being chosen by the great majority.

The French experience of initiating pupils to one foreign language at primary school was similarly considered (Favard, op cit.) to have reinforced the dominant position of English. The subsequent national report by the Ministry of Education (1996) on the first year of the new video-based approach in CE1 (children aged 7–8) found that some primary school teachers possessing competence in Spanish or Italian nonetheless taught English, thinking that English was the only option available. This led the authors of the report to ask themselves whether diversification of languages had a future.

Nagy's (op cit.) investigation of *éveil au language*, on the other hand, found no differences between the experimental and the comparison groups in relation to which languages they would prefer nor in the reasons for their choice. However, the sample was limited and the author herself cautions against reading too much into her findings. The school was situated in a migrant context, so that all pupils, including those belonging to the comparison group, were used to discussing problems of interethnicity in class. Evidence of a positive effect of the *'éveil'* approach on the status of language still needs to be gathered.

In relation to the Neandertaler Project in Italy that aimed to introduce children to three years of German, Taeschner (1991) reports that initially parents had considerable reservations and requested English instead. German is perceived by many Italians as a difficult language, but nonetheless the parents were persuaded to agree to their children learning it. After the three years, the parents had become convinced, largely because of the enthusiasm of the children and their capacity in speaking the language.

The Scottish research (Low *et al*, 1993, 1995) revealed that the introduction of four possible foreign languages (French, German, Spanish and Italian) was generally welcomed by parents and teachers, since there was no wish to 'put all the eggs in the French basket' (French traditionally having been, and remaining, by far the dominant foreign language of secondary education in Scotland). On the other hand, the diversity thereby created was not based primarily on parental choice. Decisions on which of the four languages to teach were largely reached by negotiation between national authorities, regional authorities and individual schools. Even so, this 'diversity within the system' though more easily managed than 'diversity through parental choice', nonetheless still helped create problems of continuity from primary to secondary, since teacher-supply in Italian and Spanish at secondary is not strong.

**SUMMARY**

*Societal factors:* Frequency of exposure to a foreign language varies greatly from one member state (or region) to another, so that in certain cases children begin learning a foreign language at secondary already possessing the rudiments of the language, while in other cases the lack of such exposure poses a problem not only for pupils but also for their teachers' levels of linguistic competence. Various findings suggest the beneficial effects of providing national or regional support, of ensuring quality control, of piloting schemes before implementing them more widely and of securing the involvement of parents. However, parental support may not always be spontaneously forthcoming and may have to be specifically sought in the case of minority languages or languages of perceived lower status, even if this is a language that parents speak.

*School factors:* There is general agreement concerning the importance of defining objectives, of adapting them to the realities that are experienced, and of ensuring that the children's learning of a foreign language is related to the rest of their curriculum. The difficulty of ensuring adequate continuity from one sector to another (pre-primary to primary, but particularly primary to secondary) is a handicap confirmed by several studies which suggest that lack of continuity has a negative influence on children's performance, particularly weaker or slower learners. Discontinuity may be reflected in different methods of teaching arising from ignorance among teachers in relation to traditions, possibilities and constraints operating at the other level, and weakens any potential advantage that arises from beginning a foreign language at primary. 'Time for learning' has an effect on children's performance that is confirmed by research. On the other hand no study has established a clear link between 'class size' and children's performance.

The aim of the present chapter is to describe those factors that research suggests have some influence on the outcomes that we have described in the previous chapter, and where possible to suggest what that influence is.

We considered two similar but slightly different ways of conceptualising these contextual factors.

The first way was to focus on four different types of factor, each concerned with a different set of issues:

- *Prevalent factors* that operate in a particular society or a particular community within that society, e.g. attitudes to foreign-language learning, to foreigners, to particular speech communities, the extent to which particular foreign languages are used within the society, perceptions of need for foreign languages, proximity

**SUMMARY (CONTINUED)**

*Teacher factors:* Generally, empirical studies show a link between the teacher's level of competence in the target language and the competence acquired by their pupils, especially in pronunciation and oral fluency. Not much research has been published that compares the effectiveness of different types of pre-secondary languages teachers, but the available data suggest it is preferable that teaching a foreign language at primary should be the responsibility of teachers who have been trained as primary school specialists but indispensable that they should possess a good command of the language. Where different methods/approaches have been compared, there appears to be some advantage for those geared to communication, interaction, discovery, story-telling, over more traditional approaches based on pre-constructed drills and dialogues. The diversity of approach implied by the above is not yet adequately reflected in commercial materials, since a study of their relative effectivenes which controlled for other parameters did not establish significant differences between them. Material produced by teachers themselves often seemed so similar to commercial material for another study not to have noted any differences between the two types. With regard to use of the mother tongue, its effect seems to vary according to its function. It seems to be of neutral or even negative value for everyday classroom activities but of positive value in respect of explanations and discussions of aspects that otherwise pupils would have difficulty in fully understanding. Knowledge of children's development, especially their linguistic development, seems to help teachers achieve better outcomes thanks to the judicious choice of approaches and methods that this knowledge enables them to make.

*Pupil factors:* Generally, better results appear to be attained by those pupils who tend to be good at other subjects also, with a slight tendency for girls to outperform boys. If 'length of time for learning' is held constant, there do not appear to be great differences in rate of foreign-language acquisition by different ages of beginner, though there appears to be a tendency for older beginners to learn more quickly, so that the advantage of the early start appears more connected to the overall time for learning that this makes available. Membership of minority ethnic groupings, possibly implying children who are bilingual, does not seem to have a negative influence on their learning of a foreign language and may at times benefit this process. Variations in social background on the other hand appear to have a more marked effect; however, approaches geared to the development of metalinguistic awareness appear to some extent to play a compensatory role in this respect.

to the countries where the foreign language is spoken, extent to which a particular community is characterised by social (dis)advantage. These factors can have a powerful influence on foreign-language learning. Educational decision-makers can have some influence over them but they tend to be relatively stable. However, they do change over time and even the notion of 'proximity' to another country is changing with the advent of 'virtual reality' via the Internet.

- *Provision factors* that are the result of what decision-makers choose to provide for early foreign-language learning within the educational system, e.g. the age at which the experience should start, the amount of time per week to be devoted to it, the number and types of schools to be involved initially, the number of teachers to be specially trained for the task and the nature and level of their training, the number of pupils per class, the particular aims of the initiative (tending towards learning one foreign language or towards an awakening to several). Educational decision-makers have considerable influence over these factors, and our review of the published research suggests there is considerable variation from one member state to another.

- *Process factors* reflecting the processes of teaching and learning that actually take place, e.g. teaching by a 'storytelling' or by an 'interactional' or by a 'drill and practice' method; learning by heart, by focusing on rules, by making inferences, by attempting to use the foreign language rather than simply learn it. Some of these processes are observable but others take place inside the learner's head and are therefore very difficult to identify accurately. Educational decision-makers can exercise considerable indirect influence over these factors, though not as much as with provision factors. They can, for example, strongly encourage particular methods, building them into national training programmes, or they can discourage or even proscribe other methods. Ultimately, however, the factors in this category are under the control of learners and teachers.

- *Person factors* such as an individual child's general ability, aptitude for language-learning, personality, gender, or a teacher's enthusiasm, commitment, sense of professionalism, competence in the foreign language, pedagogical skill. Educational decision-makers can have some influence over some if not all of these factors, e.g. through the ethos that they support and encourage in schools.

The second way of conceptualising the factors was to focus on the levels at which they operate, the most macro-level being that of society and the most micro being that of individual learners:

- *Factors operating at the level of society*
- *Factors operating at the level of schools*
- *Factors operating at the level of teachers*
- *Factors operating at the level of individual learners*

Both ways of representing the relevant factors have much in common, but for present purposes we have chosen this second way because of its less abstract nature.

However, before we proceed to our discussion, several words of caution are necessary, as we consider the possible relations between contextual factors and outcomes. One possible relationship is *causal,* i.e. particular factors in the context cause, or partly cause, particular outcomes. However, very few of the research studies in the present review have established, or sought to establish, this sort of relationship. Another possible relationship is *associative,* i.e. particular contextual factors tend to be associated with particular outcomes but it is not demonstrated that the one causes the other, though a statistical correlation between the two may at times be found.

There are, however, other more subtle possibilities, particularly when we bear in mind we are considering the education of young children at primary school. It would be misleading for example to assume that all of the outcomes occur only at the end of primary education. If we consider 'proficiency in the foreign language' as an outcome, we recognise that children may develop their proficiency during their all of their years at primary school, and both they and their teachers gradually become aware of this. In this sense, 'perception of outcomes of learning' is something that grows and grows rather than appearing suddenly at the end. As children proceed through primary school, this 'perception of the outcomes of learning' itself becomes a contextual factor which may influence their attitudes, self-confidence, motivation etc. With some children this cluster of factors arising from 'perception of learning' will strongly influence their further learning; with others (if there is only a weak perception of learning) it may exercise a negative influence.

What the above means is that one particular contextual factor may influence or in some way be associated with a particular outcome, or it may influence other factors in the context, thereby possibly changing these factors and possibly influencing particular outcomes as a result.

Moreover, there is considerable variation in the extent to which particular factors have been validly and reliably identified. In some cases, the researcher(s) conducting particular studies have themselves identified the factors, have provided evidence demonstrating that the particular factor is understood in the same way by other researchers and then proceeded to substantiate a relationship (whether causal or correlational) with other factors or outcomes. In other cases, however, the factors have not been identified or substantiated by the researchers, but are rather the product of teachers' and possibly pupils' unsubstantiated perceptions, with the researchers simply reporting what these are. Some of the factors that we describe in our review, e.g. 'parental involvement', 'language status' and 'knowledge of children's language development' fall into this category. In making this argument, we are not seeking to de-value particular factors but are simply pointing out that the extent to which they have been substantiated by careful research varies enormously and that considerable caution has to be adopted in interpreting their significance.

Figure 5 below presents the full list and then each factor is discussed in turn:

**Figure 5    Overview of contextual factors identified in the present research review**

| Societal factors | • Exposure to the foreign language<br>• Support for innovation and associated research<br>• Parental involvement |
|---|---|
| School factors | • Place and aims of the foreign language in the curriculum<br>• Continuity<br>• 'Time for learning'<br>• Class size |
| Teacher factors | • Training in foreign-language competence<br>• Type of teacher<br>• Strategies, methods, materials and equipment<br>• Use of mother tongue<br>• Knowledge of children's language development |
| Learner factors | • Gender<br>• Social and ethnic background<br>• Starting age<br>• General level of ability at school |

Two societal factors are discussed, with the term 'societal' being interpreted broadly to include not only society outside the educational system but also those parts of the education system, e.g. national and regional authorities that have a direct bearing on education at school but are not directly engaged in the delivery of education at school.

## Exposure to the foreign language

In the preceding chapter on 'outcomes' we already encountered an example of the effect that out-of-school exposure to the target language can achieve. According to Doyé, op cit., the success of the non-German children in the Berlin project can partly be explained by their exposure to German.

In some EU states there is relatively high exposure to a foreign language. In Holland for example before pupils begin to learn English at age 10 in primary school they have already acquired an impressive knowledge of English by means of television, radio and other media. Edelenbos (1990) reports high percentages of good answers in pre-tests at the beginning of the teaching process in respect of listening, reading and receptive vocabulary, reflecting the prior knowledge that pupils possess through exposure to the foreign language in their society. Teachers confirm that pupils begin their learning process with a firm though unstructured corpus of English.

In Germany exposure to English is the result of internationalisation of lifestyle, though films and cartoons are dubbed. Several informal counts of vocabulary have demonstrated that German Grade 3 classes may have a collective knowledge of up to 400 words of in a foreign language (e.g. Piepho, 1991). Exposure to French occurs along the South-Western German border, e.g. where there are relatives on the other side. Exposure to other languages occurs under certain local conditions, e.g. the presence of foreign-language native-speaking children in class proved beneficial because it provided many natural opportunities for spontaneous speech among peers (e.g. Sandfuchs, 1995, 1996; Riccò, 1996).

Lack of exposure to, and lack of opportunity for interaction in, the foreign language is a major factor in certain countries, e.g. in the UK. This affects not only the outcomes of foreign-language teaching at primary but also the very processes of classroom teaching, since it is not only the pupils but also their teachers who suffer from lack of language-contact. In such contexts, as the Scottish research (Low *et al*, op cit.) makes clear, there can be great difficulties in providing a supply of teachers with sufficient range, fluency, accuracy and confidence in the language and in further supporting their language development once their training has been completed. Costly training and up-dating programmes have to be set in place, since teachers in these contexts do not develop their foreign-language competence through everyday practical use outside the school.

## Support for innovation and associated research

This is a key factor in all phases of the extension of a foreign language to all primary schools in a particular country. Its role changes, depending on whether the introduction is at a relatively early phase of piloting or a fairly advanced phase of generalisation to the whole country.

The research on the national pilots in Scotland (Low *et al*, 1993, 1995) showed that the pilots were strongly supported by the Scottish Office though the appointment of additional teachers in schools and of national development officers and through the funding of a five-year research project that would feed its independent findings back into the system. At the same time, the research indicated that the education authorities at regional as well as at national levels provided substantial support through their advisory services and the convening of regular meetings of secondary and primary school staff. The overall coherence of the approach, with its high national profile, helped promote feelings of confidence, purpose and security that allowed pupils to develop certain aspects of foreign language competence which, despite certain discontinuities and shortcomings (referred to subsequently in the present section), enabled them to maintain an advantage over secondary-school beginners. Now that the pilots have been completed, it remains to be seen whether in Scotland a new infrastructure of development and research can be financed and established so as to allow the initiative to be successfully generalised across all primary schools.

In countries with a longer tradition of foreign language at primary school, e.g. Holland, the infrastructural factor was equally important. The PPON study (Vinjé, 1993) and the evaluation of primary education by the Commission for the Evaluation of Primary Education showed that children's linguistic performance was much better than anticipated. It was concluded that the core goals, especially for listening and reading, might be adjusted in order to do more justice to the actual attainments of pupils. This suggests that evaluation and research can have an influence on the national goals that are set for languages at primary school.

The existence of a collaborative network of teachers, researchers and others may be seen to have had beneficial effects when considering the Kiel, Hamburg, Wolfsburg, NorthRhine-Westphalian and Viennese studies. In Kiel the language tests for the bilingual stream were developed and modified in collaboration with experienced teachers, representing a move away from the traditional testing approach adopted in the well-known Canadian immersion programmes. Because of this consultation, the results could be interpreted in a richer way. In Wolfsburg where children with an Italian background were educated alongside German children in a project designed to help all pupils acquire competence in both German and Italian and to develop intercultural awareness, the collaborative action-research model made it possible to react to tensions among staff and to make use of strategies for intercultural team management at appropriate times (Sandfuchs, 1995, 1996; Riccò, 1996). In Bavaria, consultation during the pilot year resulted in a consolidation and reduction of the original number of aims, e.g. the aim of developing a number of modules in which other subject-content would be taught through the foreign language was not pursued (Andreas, 1996).

**Parental involvement**

In the Modena and Bolzano Projects (Lerna & Taeschner, 1991; Spadola & Taeschner, 1991) parents of children in the experimental classes were invited to allow their children to listen every day at home, and during the holidays, to a cassette with music from their foreign language lessons. This encouraged parental involvement in the children's language learning and pleasant co-operation with the teachers. In another research project in Italy, the ParLAdino project (Balboni, 1991) on the other hand parents were requested by the school to talk in the second language, Ladino, with their children, given that they were speakers of that language. However, the parents did not do so frequently, and the researcher surmises that this may have been one of the reasons that hindered success. This latter finding may be related to a substantial body of international research on the language of the home when this is a minority language within a particular state and possibly perceived as low status. Even though the school system may value this language and wish to incorporate it into children's education, it is not always the case that parents as speakers of the minority language will give their unqualified support. This phenomenon has been observed in respect of many minority languages, e.g. Scottish Gaelic.

All the German studies show a consensus among parents that primary school foreign-language learning is useful. In Bavaria the initial voluntary nature of the programme (with parents having the option of putting their children into it) was reinterpreted since all children liked to participate (Andreas, 1996).

**SCHOOL FACTORS**

### Place and aims of the foreign language in the curriculum

The concept of 'place in the curriculum' is closely tied to the amount of time available, the way the content is structured (important for continuity within the primary school and into secondary), and the links with other subjects, including embedding the foreign language within other subjects. It has already been mentioned that in Holland and Sweden national goals for English as a foreign language have been determined and national tests of children's proficiency have been designed. This enables national norms of attainment to be developed and then reviewed in the light of further research. The existence of clearly stated goals that are regularly reviewed by a national process of inspection and research helps teachers at school to gain a clear idea of what is expected. In France, which at present is at a less advanced stage of implementation, the national group of experts who wrote the Ministry of Education Report on CE1 (1996: 28) concluded it was essential to clarify the objectives. These, they argued, should go beyond the objective of sensitisation 'qui ne répond pas à l'attente des parents, des enseignants ni des enfants' (which did not correspond to the expectations of parents, teachers or children), and should include an element of actual 'language learning', however modest. They also considered it necessary to develop a teacher's guidebook that set out graded objectives, defined in terms of performance in the language. In Scotland one of the reasons adduced for the perceived success of the national pilot initiative (Low *et al*, 1993, 1995) was that it was conceived as belonging to the Scottish philosophy of primary education. For this reason, the foreign language was embedded within the five broad areas of the primary curriculum and was not taught as a separate subject that, as it were, had been imported from secondary school for children at primary.

### Continuity

The Kahl & Knebler (1996) Hamburg study showed that the experimental children maintained their advantage at secondary school. However, this finding requires further interpretation. There was evidence of a drop in the progression curve in the case of children proceeding to Gymnasium in Grade 5 because they had to cope with a new type of school. Moreover, the gap between weaker and stronger children, which tended to be hidden in Grades 3 and 4 because of the oral nature of the approach became clearer in Grade 5. However, in other types of school when the pedagogical approach of the primary school was carried over to secondary level in the orientation phase (*'Orientierungsstufe'*), the weaker children showed better progress.

The lack of continuity within primary and between primary and secondary is without doubt a major negative factor influencing outcomes. Both the Inspectorate of Schools (1991) and independent research (Edelenbos, 1993) have demonstrated that the learning processes of children in Holland were not continued when they entered secondary education. This lack of continuity may help to explain why pupils in

Holland who had experienced English at primary were only able to maintain a short-term advantage over pupils beginning at secondary, though it is additionally possible that the societal factor 'exposure to the foreign language' that was mentioned earlier may also have enabled the secondary beginners to make rapid progress and reduce the deficit. Several reasons were identified for the discontinuity between primary and secondary sectors. First, although there were regular contacts between primary and secondary schools, English as a subject and as subject-matter tended not to be discussed. Second, reciprocal classroom visits were hardly ever carried out and so there was a lack of real understanding of the different approaches used from one sector to the other. Third, there was only limited understanding at secondary level of how pupils' learning processes in respect of English at primary might be further built upon. In France, Genelot (op cit.) found that children who had been initiated in a foreign language at primary school and were subsequently placed in classes of initiated children showed a slight advantage in early secondary over initiated children placed in mixed classes (i.e. with non-initiated beginners), in respect of listening and reading comprehension written expression and cultural knowledge. However, the advantage thereby gained was not significant. A very negative impact was noted on beginners in mixed classes.

In Italy, discontinuity within the period of primary schooling, in the form of a change in methodology from a theatrical, narrative approach with young children to a more conventional form of teaching, led to de-motivation in the pupils (Taeschner, 1991). Another form of discontinuity can take the form of very long summer holidays. In some Mediterranean countries for example these can last from mid-June to mid-September, with as a consequence teachers complaining that children had forgotten a lot.

In Scotland (Low *et al*, 1993, 1995), despite the close links between primary and secondary teachers already referred to, the research identified a serious problem of discontinuity. Using a detailed classroom observation instrument, the researchers found that children in late primary were exposed to a substantially wider range of language and language topics than were pupils in early secondary where the teachers still relied heavily on existing course materials. In other words, children were not receiving sufficient opportunity for exploiting at secondary those areas of language that they had developed at primary. The researchers surmised that this may help explain the rather limited progression in foreign-language development that children appeared to make across the primary-secondary divide.

### Time for learning

Within the context of theories for explaining educational effectiveness (Carroll, 1963; Scheeren, 1992; Teddlie & Springfeld, 1993; Creemers, 1994) the time factor is seen as crucial within the school and the classroom. There are two key characteristics: 'time for learning', i.e. provision of opportunities to learn, and 'time on task', i.e. making the most of the opportunities available. The former is a 'school' factor and the latter strictly speaking a 'teacher' factor, but for present purposes both are discussed together. Of the two, 'time on task' is the key variable but can only be measured through observation of pupils, and even this can be misleading since what really counts is their unobservable mental activity. Edelenbos (1990) found that 'time for learning' was the only classroom variable that was of influence on pupils' scores for listening, reading and vocabulary, while controlling for socio-economic background. In other studies, the time factor is of influence in combination with other factors such as the use of particular types of teaching material (Vinjé, 1993), or grouping procedures (Balke, 1990). Genelot (1995) provides evidence for important practical advice given to teachers over many years: more short lessons over a long period of time improves pupils' performance. She was able to identify other characteristics of the teaching process that were also of influence, e.g. provision of explanation in the mother tongue. The same finding about the time factor is confirmed by research in Italy (Taeschner, 1986, 1991 and in press), i.e. within the same methodology a smaller number of lessons produced less good results. Children of age 8–10 who experienced two one-hour lessons per week needed three years to reach the same level of language that was attained in one year by younger children of 6–7 years who experienced 45 minutes per day for six days per week.

In France, Genelot (op cit.) identified better results in listening and reading comprehension, written expression and cultural knowledge when the overall amount of time allocated to the foreign language was substantial. The effect was less strong when the amount of time allocated was higher than 100 hours over the two years. The advantage accruing from increased time applied to higher-attaining rather than to lower-attaining pupils.

In Germany the Kiel studies (Burmeister 1994; Wode, 1996) showed that over a relatively short period of seven months the provision of two extra hours of English at Grades 5 and 6 (children aged 10 and 11) resulted in better communication skills than in the comparison group.

In comparing the Vienna Bilingual Schooling (VBS) approach with that of the Lollipop Project, Peltzer-Karpf (1996) indicated that, although both projects covered the same four-year period of primary education (Grades 1–4), there was a massive difference between the two in time and intensity. The VBS group received 1672 hours of teaching in the foreign language, plus further peer-group interaction, whereas the Lollipop children received 152 hours. In addition, a number of the VBS children were of an English-speaking family background, whereas this did not apply to the Lollipop group. These factors of time, intensity and prior knowledge clearly had a major impact on the children's acquisition of English. They offer a striking illustration of the difference between an approach based on partial immersion (VBS) and one based on the much more limited pattern of foreign language at primary school (Lollipop) that is the central concern of the present report. Even the latter pattern, given that is it based on a start in Grade 1, is at the strong end of the spectrum for foreign languages at primary school. These figures therefore caution the reader against expecting too much and emphasise the need for being clear and realistic about what to aim for in contexts where the amount of time for learning is limited.

### Class size

Research in France (Genelot, op cit.) did not find this to be a significant variable. Similar conclusions were reached elsewhere by Balke (Sweden, 1990), Edelenbos (Holland, 1990) and Vinjé (Holland, 1993).

**TEACHER FACTORS**

### Training in foreign-language competence

Two studies pertaining to teachers' foreign-language competence were conducted by Edelenbos (1990, 1993). In the 1990 study, ninety-seven teachers agreed to take tests of pronunciation and fluency in speech. The test scores of the teachers showed a positive but not statistically significant correlation with the scores of their pupils. In the 1993 study the same tests were administered to sixty primary-school teachers and sixty secondary-school teachers of English. Using the speaking scores of pupils as the dependent variable and all the teacher and teaching variables as independent variables, a step-wise regression analysis was conducted in order to determine the relative importance of the teacher and teaching variables. Of these, only one explained a significant amount of the variance in the test scores of pupils' speaking at primary school: the pronunciation and fluency of the teacher in the foreign language. The same procedure was followed with similar data from the first year of secondary education, and the analysis revealed two additional important variables: time for learning and amount of subject-matter covered. In France, Genelot (1996) found that at the end of their primary education children obtained better results when their teacher had undergone a higher level of training in the foreign language (60% of the sample having had at least two years study of English at university). The experts in France in their 1996 report to the Minister of Education (1996) surmised that those teachers who themselves had a strong affection for the foreign language they were teaching tended to be able to pass this on to their pupils.

It is worthy of note that teachers who are native speakers of what for their pupils is a foreign language obviously possess a considerable linguistic advantage. However, native-speaker teachers are not necessarily the most successful except in developing a good pronunciation in their pupils (Taeschner, 1991), partly because it may be difficult for them to understand their pupils' problems.

In Scotland (Low *et al*, 1993, 1995) teaching in the national pilots was generally undertaken by a combination of teachers from the local secondary school visiting the associated primary schools in order to work alongside the primary school classteacher. The visiting teacher from secondary supplied the foreign-language expertise while the primary teacher knew the pupils and the primary curriculum, so that each partner had something special to bring to the partnership. Now that the generalisation phase is underway, it has been judged impossible to replicate this partnership model and so large numbers of primary teachers are receiving national training in a foreign language and associated methodology. At present there is no research evidence on the outcomes of this approach.

## Type of teacher

In France, children's performance in the foreign language at primary school tended to be better when they were being taught by a primary school teacher, i.e. a person familiar with pupils and their primary school curriculum (Genelot, op cit.). This proved superior to other complementary models of teaching that had to be adopted in the initial years of the innovation, e.g. bringing in of secondary teachers and *intervenants extérieurs* who may have possessed competence in the particular language but who were not trained as primary teachers. The primary school teachers constituted 33% of the initial total sample and taught on a voluntary basis. The author emphasises that this finding is not necessarily generalisable, because the teaching was done on a voluntary basis and these volunteer teachers had undoubtedly a better command of English than did the generality of their colleagues. Moreover, it can be claimed that only 25% of them had a language training that corresponded only to the level reached by the end of secondary education. The authors of the Ministry of Education report on CE1 (1996) were convinced that 'il faut reconnaître le caractère impératif et l'urgence d'une formation linguistique et didactique pour tous les enseignants' (linguistic and didactic training for all of the teachers had to be seen as a high priority). At the time of their report, two-thirds of the teachers had received training lasting 0.5 to four days in the use of video-cassettes; 10% had participated in a more substantial period of training; and a large majority possessed only limited competence in the foreign language for which they were responsible, having to rely on what they could recall from their baccalaureate studies.

## Strategies, methods, materials, and equipment

Gangl's (1997) research in Austria found positively in favour of an interactive approach based on meaningful, narrative material which resulted in higher levels of communicative skill than in the case of children taught by means of a more conventional approach. With regard to comprehension, Gangl's research showed that when an interactive, co-operative approach was adopted, children became able to read aloud stories without preceding instructions, whereas in the more traditional approach this level would not have been reached. With regard to lexis, Gangl showed that the interactive approach (i.e. no isolated teaching of words or dialogue patterns) enabled children to develop a significantly better vocabulary than was developed through the traditional Austrian approach which focuses on dialogue patterns. Even when the aim was *éveil* rather than *initiation*, based on developing awareness pertaining to several languages, Nagy (op cit.) found that in fourth year at primary the implementation of interactive activities in groups within a class proved helpful in developing children's metalinguistic awareness.

Edelenbos (1990) found that after eliminating pupil characteristics, general instruction and certain teacher characteristics, no significant differences in oral proficiency, writing, reading listening or vocabulary remained that could be attributed to any of the particular course that had been used. Nor did the particular course have any differentiating effect on pupils' motivation. A number of projects, e.g. in Bavaria, have made use of authentic material rather than a course-book, but this is not an area that has thus far been carefully researched. In France, Genelot (op cit.) found that the use by teachers of video as a support-material helped pupils by the end of their primary education to obtain better results in listening and reading comprehension, written expression and cultural awareness. However, when video was used as the more or less exclusive source of teaching, with the teacher occupying only a facilitative role, (expert group writing for Ministry of Education in France, 1996) then this seemed to give undue emphasis to lexis, leading children to develop in their minds only a caricature of what a living language actually was, perceiving it as simply a sequence of words. At the same time, though, the authors of the Ministry of Education report considered that the children were fascinated by the video-cassettes and listened to them actively rather than passively. Nonetheless, as the year progressed a certain relaxation of their attention was noted. The authors recommended that the didactic role of the video-cassette should be emphasised, particularly by developing its possibilities for interactive exploitation.

With regard to other sorts of material, Genelot (op cit.) found there were no differences in children's attainments, depending on whether teachers used materials that had been commercially produced or that they themselves had devised.

Several research projects in Italy, e.g. Campo (1996), Lerna & Taeschner (1993) indicated that the use of a narrative approach, employing theatre, drama, role-play, story-reading and other activities that stimulate pupils' imagination produced more positive results than were produced by more conventional means. This approach also proved superior to one based on the assumption that 'play' would produce foreign-language learning in children (Taeschner, 1992). In the Bolzano project (Lerna & Taeschner, 1991), a high amount of foreign-language input from the teacher was considered to have been an important factor influencing the children's acquisition of the foreign language. In research conducted in Rome, Taeschner (1991) collected data on the acquisition of German or of English by beginners aged eight at Grade 3. The experimental group experienced an approach based on narration, acting out, mini-musicals, designed to activate processes of natural acquisition, whereas the comparison group received more conventional language teaching. The experimental group were capable of speaking spontaneously, using single words, phrases and simple sentences, some complete and others not so, some correct and others with mistakes. Their speech resembled the typical telegraphic speech of smaller children in their first language, i.e. with little use of articles or prepositions, in a large variety of different sentences. The comparison pupils on the other hand showed different linguistic behaviour, using correct short sentences learnt by heart, with little diversity of expression and much use of sentence of the kind: *'This is X'*. By the end of Grade 5 the experimental children were able to tell short stories related to stories they were acquainted with, making use of co-ordinated and subordinated sentences, whereas the comparison group were still not able to tell stories.

In their research on children aged 6–7 years in Bolzano, in which a similar story-format approach was adopted, Taeschner (op cit.) and Lerna and Taeschner (1991) found that the experimental children similarly outperformed the comparison group that began learning a foreign language one year later but received the same amount of input though on a more conventional basis. Data were collected by means of monthly individual tape-recordings. The experimental group's acquisition of German seemed to proceed through stages similar to the way monolingual small children acquire their first language. They were able to produce not only simple sentences but also bi-nuclear sentences with connectives, co-ordinate and subordinate clauses with conjunctions, arising from their story-format experience but produced in spontaneous dialogue.

A number of German studies attempted to describe the teaching process and teacher-pupil interaction by minutely analysing individual lessons. Lauerbach (1997) studied discourse patterns in a lesson using Total Physical Response. Solmecke (1997) compared three teachers' styles when teaching the same content, in order to come closer to the secret of a good lesson. Both authors point to the complexity of the process and the interplay of different factors.

## Use of the mother tongue

Genelot (op cit.) found that there was not one universal answer to the question as to whether to use the mother tongue (or the majority language of the school in schools with a number of mother tongues) in foreign-language classes. When the foreign language was being used functionally for everyday classroom activities, the use of the mother tongue was noted to have a negative effect, though not significantly so. On the other hand, when explanations were being given, the effect of using the mother tongue was positive.

Most teachers in Germany and Austria, when teaching a foreign language, try to do so by using the foreign language rather than by resorting regularly to their pupils' first language. Given the limited time available, this makes sense, though it might be a negative factor in relation to the intellectual quality of the subject-matter under discussion. Only a small amount of culture-teaching in the foreign language has been observed which would be up to the intellectual level of an 8–9 year-old, because there was a perceived taboo against use of the mother tongue (or the main language of the school).

## Knowledge of children's language development

A factor contributing to lack of success in foreign language at primary school can be inappropriate methods of teaching based on an inadequate understanding of the language-learning process. This was highlighted many years ago in the national evaluation of French at primary school in England (Burstall, 1974) in which it was reported that excessive use was made of a tape-recorder for purposes of repetition, with the consequence that a large majority of children came to 'hate the tape-recorder'. More recently, the Bolzano experiment (Lerna & Taeschner, op cit.) showed that teachers who had received appropriate training that sensitised them to children's language development tended to obtain better results.

This factor must have considerable implications for the initial and continuing education and training of primary-school teachers. What is at issue here is sensitising teachers not simply to current theories of children's foreign-language development but also to their language and cultural development more generally, and developing practical classroom approaches in which first language in standard and other varieties, second language and foreign language support and enhance rather than work against each other.

**LEARNER FACTORS**

## Gender

Vinjé (1993) reports statistically significant differences between boys and girls in their performance of learning tasks in respect of English at primary school in Holland, with girls outperforming boys. However, the data allow for no further interpretation of these differences. In Italy (e.g. Campo, 1996) girls performed better than boys but not to a significant level.

## Social and ethnic background

Studies by Edelenbos, Pyl and Vinjé (1993) compared pupils of Turkish and Moroccan origin with Dutch pupils of an equally low socio-economic status in respect of English at primary school in Holland. For the Turkish and Moroccan pupils, English was their third or fourth language, though possibly their first foreign language. In Studies 1 and 2 tests were used to assess vocabulary, reading and listening, with differences in general intelligence and level of command of Dutch between the two groups being statistically compared. No significant differences were found. In Study 3 a group of Dutch children from middle-class or upper-class backgrounds was included. The tests included vocabulary, reading, listening and fluency. There were this time no comparisons for general intelligence or command of Dutch language. No differences were found between the Turkish & Moroccan and the lower-class Dutch children, but both groups scored much lower than the middle/upper-class group. These results suggest that the possession of two or more languages by children does not of itself necessarily confer an advantage in learning a subsequent foreign language. Genelot (op cit.) however found that in France those children who at home regularly used a language other than the language of the school obtained better results in tests of listening and reading comprehension and written expression.

With regard to social background, Genelot's (op cit.) research in France found that children from socially advantaged backgrounds obtained better results than children from backgrounds that were disadvantaged. Luc (1992) on the other hand found that children from disadvantaged backgrounds were particularly receptive to language learning, when they had been introduced to two foreign languages in the fifth year of primary within an approach that emphasised metalinguistic awareness. This explicitly metalinguistic approach seemed to compensate for possible lack of prior knowledge in the case of these pupils from disadvantaged backgrounds: 'les enfants défavorisés sont particulièrement réceptifs... C'est une approche qui n'exige pas de connaissances préalables.' (Luc, 1992: 13).

In the Hamburg research (Kahl & Knebler, 1996) low social status (e.g. arising from parents out of work, single parents with lower income and refugees) was associated with lower performance in the foreign language. This factor however has to be seen as being linked to other sorts of problem, e.g. in language. In the Wolfsburg project (Sandfuchs, 1995, 1996; Riccò, 1996) the working-class Italian children had on the whole more difficulties than the German children who tended to be middle-class. In the Rhineland-Palatinate (Helfrich, 1995), teachers were invited to comment on the effects of foreign-language teaching on the children of non-German background. In the third year of the project, 65% of the teachers stated that English at Grade 3 tended to 'ease the burden'. With regard to French, an alternative foreign language that schools could opt for, the figures were 52% claiming that it eased the burden, against 48% claiming no noticeable effect.

## Starting age

Recent findings on the effects of an early start do not present a uniform picture. In the Bolzano project, Taeschner (1991) reported that the experimental children beginning at the age of six considered learning a foreign language to be easy; they found the language attractive and felt capable of speaking it. They were shown to be at ease in conversing. Children in the comparison group, who began the learning process at a later age, did not enjoy studying the foreign language to the same extent, finding it difficult. They showed more evidence of 'displacement activities' e.g. looking at the ceiling, and their motivation seemed more instrumental in that they said they had to study a foreign language since one day it would be important for their work. Seebauer (1996) on the other hand, when comparing Austrian children in Classes 1 and 3, found the Class 3 beginners to be superior in pronunciation and sound-imitation. However, Seebauer does not use this as a justification for starting a foreign language in Class 3 rather than earlier, because she argues that Classes 1 and 2 can be used in order to provide compensatory teaching that will level the differences between privileged and disadvantaged children. What is very clear is that an early start does not automatically confer major advantages. As Peltzer-Karpf's research on class 1 beginners in the Lollipop project indicates (as discussed in Chapter 2 of the present review), massive intra-group differences emerged over the first four years of instruction. For advantages to accrue, the early start factor needs to be accompanied by other factors such as 'quality of teaching' and 'time for learning'.

Since the question of the most appropriate starting age is one that undoubtedly is of interest to educational decision-makers, we judged it appropriate to add to the fairly limited picture as set out above by going back to research on this factor undertaken in the 1980s and earlier. In this connection, Burstall (1978) suggested on the basis of her review of international research that if the method of teaching and the amount of time are held constant, then older children learn more quickly than younger children. The well-known EPAL experiment in Sweden (Holmstrand, 1982) was directly concerned with the effects of starting-age. An experimental group started in Grade 1, with the comparison group starting in Grade 3. The overall total of lessons in English by the end of Grade 6 was the same for both groups. By this point there were no differences between the two groups in relation to knowledge of English, proficiency in English and attitudes towards English. In this connection it is pertinent to cite a conclusion drawn by Holmstrand from his 1982 review of the research literature: 'The results of the experimental investigations where the conditions are equivalent for the groups to be compared possess the greatest significance in this context. These results indicate unequivocally that the older subjects are superior in all the linguistic skills measured. This applies to listening comprehension, reading comprehension, vocabulary and proficiency in pronunciation' (Holmstrand, 1982: 64). We have not been able to identify any research conducted since then which makes the same comparison on an equally strict experimental basis. It is important, though, to emphasise two points. First, the advantage for older learners arises from research conducted in institutional contexts, i.e. in primary schools. The same findings would not necessarily arise in more naturalistic, non-institutional contexts where the foreign language becomes part of a child's everyday environment. Second, the advantage for older learners arises when the time for learning (between older and younger beginners) is held constant. This however deprives younger learners of perhaps their key advantage, namely the amount of time for learning the foreign language that they have at their disposal. In other words, 8-year-old beginners may indeed be ahead of 6-year-old beginners after each has had two years of foreign-language learning at school, but by the time both groups were 10, the 8-year-old beginners would be less likely to enjoy the same advantage.

We have no reason to disagree with the judgement of Singleton (1995) who in reviewing many years' international research on the age factor in learning a foreign or second language concluded that in 'naturalistic' conditions older beginners enjoy an initial advantage over younger beginners but that younger beginners tend to attain better longer-term outcomes. In institutional conditions, i.e. in schools, Singleton claims that older beginners also enjoy the initial advantage but that it can take younger beginners much longer to catch them up than in 'naturalistic' conditions, key reasons for this being that in school conditions there is less exposure to the foreign or second language and the experience is less intensive. This reminds us that in school conditions of limited exposure and non-intensive instruction there can be many breakdown points over the years and it underlines the supreme importance of the 'continuity' factor, both within the primary school and between primary and secondary levels, if the early start is indeed to confer its advantage.

## General level of ability at school

By the end of their primary education, Genelot (op cit.) found that children with a high level of performance generally, and also specifically in French as first language, obtained better results in their foreign language than those children whose general level of performance and performance in French were lower. A similar link between general ability at school and progress in foreign-language learning was established in Sweden by Balke (1990, 1991) and in Holland by Edelenbos (1990) In Italy (Taeschner, 1991) children were tested in relation to memory, attention, phonological sensitivity and mother tongue. None of these abilities on their own were shown to be decisive for acquiring a foreign language but taken together they did appear to exercise an influence. Children who scored high in all these areas were successful in their foreign language, and children scoring lower in all of these areas were also less successful in their foreign language. On the other hand, a minority of children with low cognitive scores did participate well in class and attained good results in their foreign language, suggesting that active participation in classroom language lessons was an important a factor.

# 5 RECOMMENDATIONS

The two preceding chapters take stock of the outcomes of learning and experiencing languages at primary school (Chapter 3) and of those factors that recent research suggests may have some influence on these outcomes (Chapter 4).

On this basis the present writers have elaborated ten recommendations which they consider appropriate for future action. The first seven derive directly from the contextual factors outlined in Chapter 4. The last three are more general in nature and take account of data presented in Chapter 3.

In order to formulate the recommendations which flow from our analysis of the contextual factors, we shall take each level in turn: society, schools, teachers, learners. Each factor identified will be examined from three perspectives: a) its potential influence on outcomes, b) an indication of any shortcomings that may be detected in respect of this factor in the majority of situations at present, and c) such possibilities as may suggest themselves for intervention. The order in which the recommendations appear is not hierarchical but simply corresponds to the order in which they appear in Chapter 4. A hierarchical organisation would in any case have been difficult to establish, since the shortcomings (point b) and the possibilities for intervention (point c) undoubtedly vary from one situation to another.

## RECOMMENDATIONS PERTAINING TO FACTORS AT THE LEVEL OF SOCIETY

The first level of factor reviewed in Chapter 4 was the societal level. The extent to which pupils were or were not 'exposed to a foreign language outside of school' was identified as a factor that facilitates or hinders children's foreign-language development. Exposure is linked to the place and status of the language within the community to which pupils belong, their neighbouring communities or the media. Two types of intervention may in principle be envisaged: by increasing out-of-school exposure (essentially through the media and increasingly the Internet) to the language that has been chosen for instruction, or by taking account of existing levels of exposure to particular languages in making the choice in the first place of which foreign language(s) to teach. In both cases, the action envisaged may possibly serve to reinforce the already dominating position of particular languages. Accordingly no recommendation may be made without reference to more global perspectives of languages policy. That is why our recommendation in respect of exposure will be integrated with Recommendation 8.

### Recommendation 1

Chapter 4 highlights the positive role played by a national or regional infrastructure that supports innovation and associated research. The reflections of experts involved in the implementation and evaluation of foreign languages in primary schools in several European countries (c.f. Doyé & Hurrell, 1997) also emphasise this same point.

In the past, in various countries at various stages of development, the infrastructure of support was satisfactory in some cases but inadequate, not to mention highly deficient, in others. One of the most common features of these earlier initiatives was to provide an adequate, sometimes very good, infrastructure during the phase of piloting but to reduce the level of support and possibly even to change the basic parameters of the situation at the crucial point of generalisation of the initiative across the country. In fact, the generalisation phase is one in which the possibility of intervention is essential, which has implications for the levels of financial support that will be necessary.

Admittedly, a highly professional infrastructure for innovation and associated research is expensive, but at every stage it can benefit the system by feeding relevant knowledge and experience into initial teacher education (ITE) or the continuing professional development (CPD) of practising teachers.

**Therefore:**

### Recommendation 1

**At every phase of the planning, implementation and subsequent adaptation of foreign-language teaching in pre-primary or primary education, sufficient funding should be made available for supporting innovation and associated research. The infrastructure that is put in place may vary according to the particular phases of an initiative, but it should always focus on evaluation of the outcomes that have been obtained and the support given to teachers' involvement, and on the interaction between these two elements.**

## Recommendation 2

No empirical studies among those analysed deal with the effect of 'parental involvement' in the specific domain of foreign language-learning at school, and so we were able to gather only limited evidence on this factor. However the assumption of its positive role is supported by several research studies that deal with education more generally (e.g. Kellaghan, Sloane, Alvarey and Bloom, 1993). In principle the situation seems favourable, since public opinion which is generally aware of the increasing needs to communicate with partners who speak other languages, is itself generally in favour of teaching foreign languages. Problems may begin to appear when attempts are made to teach languages other than those that are major, dominant international languages and that parents are already convinced their children should learn, and serious misunderstandings can arise with regard to the objectives that a school may set for the teaching that it provides. There are many means of intervening on this aspect, both at the macro-sociological level (explanations given by the national media) and at the micro-sociological level (through direct links between schools and parents).

**Therefore:**

### Recommendation 2

**In the course of the introduction of a foreign language at primary school, parental involvement is important. This involvement should rest on helping parents to achieve a clear understanding of the objectives pursued by the school. Involving parents will establish an encouraging, supportive environment outside the classroom in which children may talk about, study and use the foreign language they are learning. It will also give the school an opportunity for discussing with parents and sensitising them in respect of any language-choices that may be available.**

**RECOMMENDATIONS
PERTAINING TO FACTORS
AT THE LEVEL OF SCHOOLS**

## Recommendation 3

Within the level of 'school factors' the main element for which clear evidence could be gathered from the empirical research that we reviewed is 'continuity'. Mostly, the research-focus has been on continuity from primary to secondary. It shows that discontinuity has a negative influence on pupil performance. Unfortunately, there are no studies available with an appropriate design that point clearly to the various educational variables that could enhance continuity. Although discontinuity between primary and secondary education will present itself in different forms throughout Europe, it is possible to identify five elements which most situations share in common: a) a communication gap between staff (managers and teachers) involved in primary and secondary education; b) a lack of fine-turning and compatibility of aims, at several intermediate stages; c) differences in approaches, in topics covered and in linguistic insight; d) reluctance at the secondary level to acknowledge the learning that has taken place at primary; and e) shortcomings in initial teacher education and in provision for teachers' continuing professional development to address the above mentioned problems. It is true that 'discontinuity' is a well-attested phenomenon that can affect all or most aspects of a school's curriculum, but it can have a particularly negative effect on children's foreign-language development, since there is abundant evidence to suggest how fragile their interim and slowly developing competence in a foreign language can be and how difficult it often is to transfer this fragile competence from one known context to another that is not known and is very different. In each of these domains, effective intervention is both possible and highly desirable.

**Therefore:**

**Recommendation 3**

**Pedagogical continuity should be ensured across the different sectors of education (pre-primary, primary and secondary) that children experience. Teachers, teacher educators, school managers, researchers and key persons of influence in each member state should make a joint effort in analysing the problems of continuity in as detailed a fashion as possible, with reference both to foreign-language teaching and to education more generally. They should develop and implement various means of intervention in those domains where discontinuity is apparent. The initial and continuing education of teachers should alert them to the problems involved: it should enable them to consider in a well-informed way children's progression throughout the entire course of their education and to collaborate with colleagues at previous or subsequent levels of education.**

## Recommendation 4

The empirical studies examined in Chapter 4 clearly highlight the importance of the amount of time allocated to learning a foreign language. Indeed, the 'time factor' seems to be the most reliable predictive classroom-related factor for explaining differences in pupils' foreign-language learning (Edelenbos and Johnstone, 1996). The current situation is characterised by considerable variation, both in respect of the amount of time allocated to foreign-language learning each week, the frequency and length of lessons and the overall quantity and distribution of time throughout the pre-primary and primary education period. So far as the overall amount of time is concerned, it is clear that the possibilities for intervention are limited, with children's timetables already being full and with any increase of time in favour of languages tending to be perceived as being at the expense of other areas of children's curriculum. Any limitation of time will affect all four language modes of listening, speaking, reading and writing, but our review shows clear evidence (even in countries where there is relatively good exposure to a foreign language through the various media) that the mode which develops most slowly is speaking. If pupils are to develop an ability to be creative, fluent and reasonably accurate and wide-ranging in their talk, then substantial time must be allowed. However, the specific outcomes of certain empirical studies in our review make it possible to envisage actions that could be both realistic and effective. It became evident that the specific effect of 'time for learning' became clear only in combination with other contextual factors related to the quality of teaching. It was also found in one study that the effect of increasing the length of time became less important above a certain number of hours and other studies suggest that the distribution of the overall amount of time available into shorter, more frequent lessons yields better results. It is essentially on this evidence that we base our fourth recommendation.

**Therefore:**

**Recommendation 4**

**Foreign-language teaching in pre-primary and primary education, to be effective, takes time. It is therefore recommended that the overall amount of time made available for it should be increased, wherever this is possible. However, simply increasing the 'time for learning' will not guarantee improved results. It has to be combined with attempts to improve the quality of teaching and of learning. Where possible, there should be short but frequent (in principle, daily) lessons rather than one or two longer lessons per week.**

**RECOMMENDATIONS PERTAINING TO FACTORS AT THE LEVEL OF TEACHERS**

**Recommendation 5**

With regard to 'teacher factors' the empirical research reviewed in Chapter 4 allows several elements to be highlighted that testify to the importance of appropriate teacher education, both

- directly in respect of their command of the language (particularly their oral command) and their knowledge of children's language development, and also

- indirectly through the knowledge that certain approaches can achieve better results. This however pre-supposes teachers who have received appropriate training and support in matters such as planning for and coping with change, maintaining an innovation once it has been launched and the first flush of success has worn off, and self-evaluation.

It is worthy of note that both aspects are closely related to each other: the new methodological approaches set out in Chapter 4 all involve interactive language use between teacher and pupils. It is not possible for this to occur unless the teacher possesses an appropriate level of confidence and fluency in the language. Moreover, in order to be able to take account of the diverse and evolving interests and needs of children, it is important that teachers should be able to draw spontaneously and flexibly on a variety of different themes rather than rely on language they have more or less learnt by heart for dealing with situations that are simply routine and predictable.

The tendency at present is to allocate the teaching of a foreign language at pre-primary and primary school to teachers who specialise in teaching at these levels. There are many arguments in favour of this, and we consider that the research we have reviewed tends to confirm the efficacy of this approach, provided that the teachers have received an adequate preparation for the specific task. In contrast to their colleagues in secondary schools, primary school teachers are generally not specialised in a foreign language and its teaching. They therefore have very important training needs, whether these relate to enhancing the training that as practising teachers they have already received or to the further development during initial teacher education of the language skills they acquired when at school. In this regard, there are serious shortcomings at present. In most countries in which it has been decided to generalise the pre-secondary teaching of a foreign language, the degree of support for training a sufficient number of teachers to the appropriate level of language competence falls well below any level that would have to be attained in order to offer good prospects of success.

Once again, this is a domain where positive intervention is possible, provided that the means are made available. It is also worthy of note that having recourse to specialist language teachers who have been trained to teach at secondary does not eliminate the need for training, since in these cases it becomes important to induct them into the pedagogy of pre-primary and primary education and the didactics of language-teaching at these levels.

**Therefore:**

**Recommendation 5**

**Teachers should be educated in the following domains: proficiency in the target language; description of this language, including comparison with the mother tongue (and/or with the majority language of the school); processes of first and second language acquisition; pedagogy for pre-primary and primary education and for language teaching at these levels. Depending on the prior experiences and qualifications of particular individuals, these components may already be acquired, to a greater or lesser extent. In respect of these other components which have not yet been acquired, it would be ill-advised to settle for a 'light' induction lasting only a few hours. On the contrary, substantial courses will be needed.**

**This training/education would lead teachers a) to develop a good command of the foreign language, b) to acquire a capacity for analysing linguistic phenomena and a knowledge of children's language development. This would allow them to observe, understand, correct and improve children's progress in learning a foreign language and in so doing would enable children themselves to gain some insights into language-related phenomena, and c) to play an active part in pedagogical innovation, in collaboration with any didactic research that was taking place at the time.**

**RECOMMENDATIONS PERTAINING TO FACTORS AT THE LEVEL OF LEARNERS**

**Recommendation 6**

As far as 'learner factors' are concerned, empirical research enables us to claim that a child's general level of verbal ability at school is of major importance for learning a foreign language. 'General level of ability' is an umbrella concept about which there is an absence of coherent theory. In empirical research it is often operationalised as an intelligence score or in relation to some other psychometric indicator, and sometimes more broadly in respect of high, middle and lower performing children. In various empirical studies, comparisons of verbal intelligence scores and performance in learning a foreign language usually achieve a positive correlation. Even though these correlations vary considerably, this suggests that a factor such as 'general verbal ability' probably does have a strong influence an foreign language outcomes. There is also some evidence for a 'gender factor', in that there is a slight tendency for girls to out-perform boys in foreign languages by the end of primary education. Other empirical studies indicate that a more modest social-class background is often related to lower levels of outcome, whereas ethnic origin and the bilingualism that results from this tend not to constitute a handicap and can even have a positive influence on children's foreign-language performance.

If we take stock of the above mentioned factors in relation to shortcomings in the system and possibilities for intervention, the 'gender' factor does not appear to be a great cause for concern, though in some contexts it may be important to focus on differences in attitude and performance between boys and girls. So far as 'general verbal ability' and 'social class background' are concerned, we are led back to a more general problem within educational systems which consists of enabling the totality of children within a system to receive an adequate and appropriate education, and in particular to reduce the educational inequalities (and inequities) which appear to be closely linked to social inequality (c.f. Langouet, 1994). (For an analysis of links between low attainments in languages, low performance more generally at school and social-class background, c.f. Candelier and Hermann-Brennecke, 1993). Our general recommendation would of course be to develop global policies for schools that would be likely to reduce these fundamental types of inequality, but recommendations may be formulated which concern our specific domain.

**Therefore:**

### Recommendation 6

**It is appropriate to encourage research and innovation that aims to elaborate didactic approaches such that those children who generally experience difficulties at school and/or who are from a disadvantaged social-class background may have the best possible opportunities for success in learning a foreign language during the pre-secondary phase. This additional area of learning must not become for this particular group of learners yet another occasion for experiencing failure. Ways should be found of enhancing the motivation, curiosity and interest of boys and thereby influencing their subsequent attainments. Children from bi- or multi-lingual minority groups should not be excluded from learning a foreign language at primary school on grounds of alleged pedagogical learning difficulties that arise from their specific situation.**

### Recommendation 7

Empirical evidence illustrated in Chapter 4 shows that research has not definitively established an 'optimum age' for starting a foreign language at school. An early start offers a longer period for learning overall and has the potential to influence children's personal development when they are still at a highly formative stage. However, the earlier the start, the greater the importance of continuity from one year to another. On its own, an early start will be unlikely to make a substantial difference. Its chances of doing so will be increased if it is associated with other factors such as 'quality of teaching' from teachers who have developed the range of knowledge and skills outlined in Recommendation 5.

**Therefore:**

**Recommendation 7**

**Innovation in respect of teaching a foreign language should not be reduced to simply lowering the age at which children begin. A measure of this sort does not of itself constitute a pedagogical solution. It is of great importance to develop appropriate methodologies that are in tune with the needs of each age-group. To make this assertion is not to contradict the notion of 'continuity' contained in Recommendation 3 but simply to state that the differences which gradually appear from one level of pre-primary and primary education to another should be understood and respected.**

**RECOMMENDATIONS ARISING FROM BROADER CONSIDERATIONS OF DIVERSITY, RESEARCH AND INNOVATION**

We now arrive at our final three recommendations which are not tied so directly to the factors reviewed in Chapter 4 but which arise from our text as a whole, including our discussion of outcomes in Chapter 3.

**Recommendation 8**

Regrettably there have not been any empirical studies directly concerned with the effects that the introduction of a foreign language during pre-primary or primary education can have on the diversity of the languages that are taught and learnt. It was noted nonetheless at the end of Chapter 3 that various indicators suggest these effects can be perceived as negative. A purely mathematical argument can be advanced in support of this view: since in most countries primary and pre-primary schools are smaller than secondary schools, starting a foreign language at primary can lead to the selection of the foreign language from a narrower range. Moreover, an earlier start in learning a foreign language can reinforce the position of that language which tends to be a dominant majority language, thereby adding further to the disequilibrium.

**Therefore:**

**Recommendation 8**

**Where linguistic diversity is the aim, careful consideration should be given as to how this may be achieved. One possible means of encouraging diversity is to allow for choice of language to be learnt at primary, in which case care should be taken to allow an actual choice between a number of languages and/or to balance the advantage given to one language through new measures in favour of additional languages at secondary. However, the provision of 'choice' (whether by parents and their children or by schools) does not by itself guarantee diversity. The implications of 'choice' need to be carefully thought through, particularly in relation to the provision of teachers of a less widely used language, if continuity in the chosen language from primary and through secondary is to be maintained. Another solution could be to encourage an 'awakening' to several languages instead of an 'initiation' to one language, an approach that conveys potential benefits but that needs further evaluation. In order to take advantage of the positive effects of exposure to a target language out-of-school without reinforcing the**

position of languages that are already dominant in the media, there is merit in favouring those languages that are present in the environment or in neighbouring regions. Programmes which allow for regular encounters by classes of pupils situated in the vicinity of linguistic frontiers should be encouraged and developed.

## Recommendation 9

Our aim of gathering empirical data that was reliable and validated by research revealed how small in number and lacking in variety were research projects of this sort, whether focusing on the outcomes of pre-secondary education or on the factors that might influence these outcomes. From such evidence as we have been able to gather, the research effort has not matched the level of interest within public opinion or among those who act as educational decision-makers. This applies not only to research based on evaluation studies but also to research that has analysed the processes of acquisition and learning and to action-research which allows new didactical approaches to be elaborated. Several of the factors brought together in Chapter 4 have a direct link with research, with the consequence that research has been already referred to in recommendations already mentioned. However, it seems to us essential that we should devote a recommendation to this aspect.

Moreover, considering that many important questions about the role of particular contextual factors remain unanswered and that many educational authorities have found difficulty in providing the basic conditions for success in foreign-language teaching in primary schools, it seemed to us necessary to sound a note of caution against over-reliance on one particular formula for offering a foreign language in pre-primary or primary education. Research has a vital role to play in promoting a spirit of critical reflection that challenges received and dominant views, though other complementary routes drawing for example on modes of imaginative thinking or problem-solving must of course also be explored.

**Therefore:**

**Recommendation 9**

**It is strongly recommended that research should be commissioned in relation to the evaluation of outcomes and the links between outcomes and contextual factors, to the study of processes of acquisition and learning and to pedagogical innovation. While leaving scope for the initiatives of researchers themselves, it seems essential that there should be an overall coordination such that the various domains of research are effectively covered and a genuine synergy created. The questions which persist in relation to certain conditions that are essential for success in offering a foreign language in pre-primary and primary education and the difficulties encountered in numerous contexts in achieving a successful implantation imply that the door should be left open for implementing and carefully evaluating alternative solutions, such as incorporating the 'language awareness' approach which has also been taken into account in the present review. Indeed a major challenge for the future might be to identify, investigate and further refine appropriate formulae that combined the merits of awakening children to a variety of languages with the merits of enabling them to make good progress in one or more than one of these at pre-secondary and/or secondary level.**

**Recommendation 10**

European citizens should be able to understand people speaking languages other than their mother tongue. In particular, favourable situations children can easily learn to speak and to understand one or more languages: those who grow up in bilingual families often become near-native speakers of both languages; and pupils who are educated in a school where a language other than the mother tongue is the main language of instruction will under certain conditions tend to become very fluent.

However it is also important to provide for the very much larger number of children in more common situations really good opportunities for acquiring a worthwhile level of proficiency in one or more foreign languages. While Edelenbos, Starren and Welsing (1997) in a review of early foreign-language teaching and learning found no evidence to point to negative effects on pupils, it is undoubtedly true that over-ambitious or inadequately planned and resourced initiatives can lead parents, teachers and possibly pupils to feel frustrated and let down, all the more so since the notion of languages for young learners tends to generate ambitious expectations in the first place. Our review has shown that success in this regard depends on a range of factors which we have attempted to enumerate as precisely as possible. As already implied in Recommendation 7, it would be unwise to expect miracles from the mere fact that the learners are children.

**This therefore leads to our tenth and final recommendation:**

**Recommendation 10**

**If the minimal conditions for the factors outlined earlier in our text are not fulfilled, the inefficiency of those measures that are adopted may well provoke disenchantment among parents, teachers and even pupils, thereby preventing pupils from making progress in acquiring the particular language(s) they are learning and in developing the sense of linguistic and cultural diversity that early language learning can promote. This need to provide the minimal conditions is vital, precisely because the very notion of early language learning has a tendency to raise hopes and expectations in parents and others to an unrealistic level. That is why we recommend that, before taking decisions concerning the implementation and especially the generalisation of foreign-language teaching in primary or earlier education, decision-makers should first of all ascertain that they can provide the minimal conditions which will ensure that the aspirations of those involved in this educationally invaluable enterprise are fulfilled.**

*Christiane Blondin* is a researcher within the *Service de Pédagogie expérimentale* at the University of Liège. She has researched a variety of educational topics, and her language interests include second-language immersion and foreign-language teaching.

*Michel Candelier* teaches the didactics of French as a foreign language at the University René Descartes, Paris 5. His research interests include the teaching of grammar (first/second-language) and the articulation of didactics and language policy within a perspective of linguistic pluralism.

*Peter Edelenbos* is member of GION, the Institute for Educational Research at the University of Groningen. His research interests cover a range of educational and vocational topics and he has conducted a number of evaluation studies of English at primary school.

*Richard Johnstone* is Professor of Education at the University of Stirling and Director of the Scottish Centre for Information on Language Teaching and Research. He has directed several research projects on language-learning for the Scottish Office.

*Angelika Kubanek-German* lectures on the didactics of English in the Department of Language and Literature, Catholic University of Eichstätt. Her specialist research interests are in foreign languages at primary school, bilingual education and intercultural learning.

*Traute Taeschner* is Professor at the University of Rome 'La Sapienza' where her specialist research interests are in psycholinguistics, bilingualism and the development of second and foreign languages in children within pre-school and primary education.

Each of the authors contributed to the selection and analysis of the empirical studies that form the basis of the text. Michel Candelier and Christiane Blondin accepted responsibility for processing the research studies published in French; Richard Johnstone and Peter Edelenbos for those in English; Peter Edelenbos for those published in Holland and Sweden; Angelika Kubanek-German for the substantial body of research in German; Traute Taeschner for studies emanating from southern Europe and those featuring pre-school education. The framework for analysis, which is given in the Appendix, was developed and applied by the full team, but particular responsibility for its elaboration was undertaken by Michel Candelier who also drafted the Introduction. Richard Johnstone drafted Chapters 2, 3 and 4 and assembled the bibliography. The recommendations were drafted by Peter Edelenbos, Michel Candelier and Christiane Blondin. Michel Candelier with the support of Christiane Blondin was responsible for the overall editing of the text, and Richard Johnstone for its eventual expression in English.

However, with the benefit of meetings supported by DG22 of the European Commission, enhanced considerably by prior and subsequent interaction via electronic mail, all members of the team worked together in order to elaborate the present text from the initial draft versions. There are diverse views about the aims and approaches appropriate for foreign languages in primary schools and pre-school education. We authors reflect this diversity and indeed, even now that our study is completed, we do not fully share one common view. However, we see this diversity as an advantage in that it has enabled us to look at the data from more than one perspective and to negotiate meanings in order to assume joint responsibility for our text.

# THE FRENCH AND GERMAN VERSIONS

The text was not conceived in any one single language. The meetings of the team of authors were conducted multilingually. When it came to drafting the text, some parts were drafted in French, others in German and others in English. From this, the first monolingual version to be written was the present one in English.

The French version is provisionally entitled:

> *Les langues étrangères dès l'école primaire ou maternelle: quels résultats, à quelles conditions?*

The German version is provisionally entitled:

> *Fremdsprachen für die Kinder Europas: Ergebnisse und Empfehlungen der Forschung.*

and is due to be published by Cornelsen Verlag, Berlin.

It is hoped that an Italian version will also be published.

Further detail on the published versions in languages other than English may be sought from Scottish CILT: Fax: (0)1786 46 7631 or e-mail LG1@stir.ac.uk

CiLT

# REFERENCES

ANDREAS, R. (1996). *Fremdsprachen in der Grundschule: Ziele, Unterricht und Lernerfolge. Ergebnisse der Begleituntersuchungen.* München: Institut für Schulpaedagogik und Bildungsforschung.

BAILLY, D. & LUC, C. (1992). Approche d'une langue étrangère à l'école. *Études psycholinguistiques et aspects didactiques.* (Vol 2). Paris: INRP.

BALBONI, P.E. (1991). Il Progetto ParLAdino. *Educazione bilingue.* 91–134.

BALKE, G. (1990). *Engelska i Arskurs 5: Resultat fran insamlingen inom den nationella utvärderingen av grundskolan. NUengelska 3.* Göteborgs Universitet: Institutionen för pedagogik.

BALKE, G. (1991). *Multilevel factor analysis of proficiency in English as a foreign language.* Paper presented at the symposium Multilevel factor analysis: Applications to Education. Annual meeting of American Educational Research Association, Chicago.

BURMEISTER, P. (1994). *English im Bili-Vorlauf: Pilotstudie zur Leistungsfähigkeit des verstärkten Vorlaufs in der 5. Jahrgangsstufe deutsch-englisch bilingualer Zweige in Schleswig-Holstein.* Kiel.

BURSTALL, C. et al. (1974). *Primary French in the balance.* Slough: National Foundation for Educational Research.

BURSTALL, C. (1978). Factors affecting foreign-language learning: a consideration of some recent research findings. In: KINSELLA, V. (Ed) *Language Teaching and Linguistic Surveys.* Cambridge University Press.

CAMPO, O. (1996). A scuola si raccontano le favole. Un'esperienza didattica col format. Tesi di Laurea, Facoltà di Psicologia, Università di Roma 'La Sapienza'.

CANDELIER, M. & HERMANN-BRENNECKE, G. (1993). *Entre le choix et l'abandon: les langues étrangères à l'école, vues d'Allemagne et de France.* Paris: Didier & Crédif [Collection Essais].

CARROLL, J.B. (1963). A model of school learning. *Teachers College Record, 64,* 723–733.

CHARMEUX, E. (1992). Maîtrise du français et familiarisation avec d'autres langues. *Repères, 6,* 155–172.

CREEMERS, B.P.M. (1994). *The effective classroom.* London: Cassell.

DE LEEUW, H. (1995). Über die Angst beim Fremdsprachenlernen in der Grundschule. In: BREDELLA, L. & CHRIST, H. (Eds) *Didaktik des Fremdverstehens.* Tübingen: Narr, 170–185.

DE LEEUW, H. (1997). *English as a foreign language in German elementary schools. What do the children think?* Tübingen: Narr.

DJIGUNOVICH, J. M. (1995). Attitudes of young foreign-language learners: a follow-up study. In: Vilke, M. (Ed) *Children and foreign languages.* Zagreb: University of Zagreb, Faculty of Philosophy, 16–33.

DOYÉ, P. (1997). Bilinguale Grundschulen. *Zeutschrift für Fremdsprachenforschung, 8,* 161–195.

EDELENBOS, P. (1990). *Leergangen voor Engels in het basisonderwijs vergeleken.* Dissertation University of Groningen. Groningen: RION.

EDELENBOS, P. (1993). *De aansluiting tussen Engels in het basisonderwijs en Engels in het voo rtgezet onderwijs.* Eindrapport SVO-project 0015. Groningen: RION.

EDELENBOS, P. & JOHNSTONE, R. (eds) (1995). *Researching languages at primary school. Some European perspectives.* London: Centre for Information on Language Teaching and Research.

EDELENBOS, P., STARREN, P. & WELSING, W. (1997). *Vroegtijdig vreemde talenonderwijs: synthese van een inventarisatie van Europese projecten.* Maastricht: Talenacademie Nederland.

EDELENBOS, P., PIJL, Y.J. & VINJE, M.P. (1993). *Verschillen in het beheersingsniveau van het Engels tussen allochtone en autochtone leerlingen.* Groningen: RION.

FAVARD, J. (1992). Les langues étrangères à l'école primaire: la problématique française. In: ARNSDORF, D., BOYLE, H., CHAIX, P. & O'NEIL, C. (eds). *L'apprentissage des langues étrangères à l'école primaire.* Paris: Didier Érudition. 29–38.

FAVARD, J. (1993). L'initiation aux langues étrangères à l'école primaire: bilan de trois années d'apprentissage. *Bulletin de l'ADEAF,* (43), 8–12.

GANGL, R. (1997). *Learning through interaction – a discourse model for FLT to primaries.* Manuscript: unpublished doctoral thesis, Karl-Franzens-Universität, Graz.

GENELOT, S. (1996). *L'enseignement des langues à l'école primaire: quels acquis pour quels effets au collège? Éléments d'évaluation: le cas de l'anglais* (Les Notes de l'Iredu). Dijon: Institut de Recherche sur l'Économie de l'Éducation.

GOMPF, G. (1996). *Englisch gehört zu meinen Lieblingsfächern.* Wissenschaftliche Untersuchung der Einstellung von Viertklässern zum Lernbereich Englisch. Jahrbuch 96 des Fördervereins 'Kinder lernen europäische Sprachen', 85–93. Stuttgart.

GROUPE NATIONAL D'EXPERTS (FRANCE) (1996). *L'initiation à une langue au cours élémentaire, première annèe. Rapport d'étape.* Paris: Ministère de l'Éducation.

HAENISCH, H. & THÜRMANN, R. (1995). *Begegnung mit Sprachen in der Grundschule. Eine empirische Untersuchung zum Entwicklungsstand, der Akzeptanz und zu den Realisierungsformen von Begegnung mit Sprachen in den Grundschulen Nordrhein-Westfalens.* Soest: Landesinstitut fur Schule und Weiterbildung.

HELFRICH, H. (1995). Evaluation des Modellversuchs 'Integrierte Fremdspracharbeit an Grundschulen in Rheinland-Pfalz'. In: Staatliches Institut fur Lehrerfort- und -weiterbildung: *Entwicklung und Erprobung eines didaktischen Konzepts zur Fremdsprachenarbeit in der Grundschule.* Abschlußbericht. Speyer, 97–122.

HOLMSTRAND, L.S.E. (1982). *English in the elementary school.* Stockholm/Uppsala: Almqvist & Wiksell International.

KELLAGHAN, T., SLOANE, K., ALVAREZ, B. & BLOOM, B.S. (1993). *The Home Environment and School Learning. Promoting Parental Involvement in the Education of Children.* San Francisco: Jossey-Bass.

KUBANEK-GERMAN, A. (1996). *Kindgemäßer Fremdsprachenunterricht. Zur Entwicklung eines Leitbegriffs früh beginnender fremdsprachlicher Lehre.* Habilitationsschrift, Sprach- und Literaturwissenschaftliche Fakultät der Katholischen Universität Eichstätt.

INSPECTIE VAN HET ONDERWIJS (1991). *Engels in de basisschool en de brugklas.* Zoetermeer: Inspectie van het onderwijs.

KAHL, P. & KNEBLER, U. (1996). *Englisch in der Grundschule, und dann? Evaluation des Hamburger Schulversuchs.* Berlin: Cornelsen.

LANGOUËT, G. (1994). *La démocratisation de l'enseignement aujourd'hui.* Paris, ESF.

LANDESINSTITUT FÜR SCHULE UND WEITERBILDUNG (1995). *Lernen für Europa. Abschlußbericht eines Modellversuchs.* Soest: Landesinstitut für Schule und Weiterbildung.

LAUERBACH, G. (1997). Fünf Mikro-Analysen unterrichtlicher Interaktion aus dem Goethe-Institut Projekt 'Sprachbrücke'. In: LEGUTKE, M. (Ed.) *Unterrichtsforschung Fremdsprachenlernen Primarbereich.* (In Press).

LERNA, A. & TAESCHNER, T. (1993). *Progetto Europeo di cooperazione: L'insegnamento della seconda lingua a bambini dai 3 ai 10 anni.* Rapporto Tecnico, Università degli Studi di Roma 'La Sapienza'.

LERNA, A. & TAESCHNER, T. (1991). *Sperimentazione 'Tedesco nelle prime elementari'.* Rapporti Tecnici n. 1, 2, 3 e 4, Università degli Studi di Roma 'La Sapienza'.

LOW, L., DUFFIELD, J., BROWN, S. & JOHNSTONE, R. (1993). *Evaluating foreign languages in Scottish primary schools. Report to Scottish Office.* Stirling: Scottish CILT.

LOW, L., BROWN, S., JOHNSTONE, R. & PIRRIE, A. (1995). *Foreign languages in Scottish primary schools – Evaluation of the Scottish pilot projects: Final Report to Scottish Office.* Stirling: Scottish CILT.

LUC, C. (1992). *Approche d'une langue étrangère à l'école. Perspectives de l'apprentissage* (Vol 1). Paris: INRP.

MITCHELL, R., MARTIN, C. & GRENFELL, M. (1992). *Evaluation of the Basingstoke primary schools language awareness project: 1990/91.* University Southampton Centre for Language Education, Occasional Paper 7.

CILT

NAGY, C. (1996). *L'éveil au langage: contribution à une étude de l'activité métalangagière de l'enfant à l'école élémentaire.* (Thèse de Doctorat). Grenoble.

PELZ, M. & BAUER, E. (1990). Bilinguale Erziehung in einer Grenzregion. Kommunikation von Grundschulkindern in zweisprachigen Kontakten. *Neusprachliche Mitteilungen,* 43, 15–17.

PELTZER-KARPF, A., DRINGEL-TECHT, E., JANTSCHER, E. & ZANGLE, R. (1996). *Vienna Bilingual Schooling. Die vierte Klasse.* Karl-Franzens-Universität, Graz.

PELTZER-KARPF, A., HASIBA, U. & ZANGL, R. (1996). *Lollipop-Programm: Psycholinguistische Untersuchung zur vierten Klasse.* Report. Karl-Franzens-Universität, Graz.

PELTZER-KARPF, A. & NEUMANN, A. (1996). *Vienna Bilingual Schooling: A start in a new language. Pragmalinguistische Ergänzungsstudie. Zur Interaktion in den ersten Wochen des VBS Unterrichts.* Karl-Franzens-Universität, Graz.

PETILLON, H. (1995). Integrierte Fremdsprachenarbeit in der Grundschule aus der Perspektive der beteiligten Kinder – eine Pilotstudie. In: Staatliches Institut für Lehrerfort- und -weiterbildung (Ed) *Entwicklung und Erprobung eines didaktischen Konzepts zur Fremdsprachenarbeit in der Grundschule. Abschlußbericht.* Speyer, 141–153.

PIEPHO, H.-E. (1991). *Englisch in der Grundschule.* Bochum: Kamp.

PINTO, M.A. (1993). Le dévelopement métalinguistique chez les infants bilingues. Problématiques théoriques et résultats de recherche. *Scientia Paedagogica Experimentalis,* xxx, 1, 119–148.

PINTO, M.A., TAESCHNER, T. & TITONE, R. (1995). Second Language Teaching in Italian Primary Education. In EDELENBOS, P. & JOHNSTONE, R. (Eds) *Researching Languages at Primary School: Some European Perspectives.* Stirling: Scottish CILT.

RICCÒ, A. (1996). *Italienischunterricht in der Deutsch-Italienischen Grundschule Wolfsburg.* Manuscript. Hannover.

SANDFUCHS, U. (1995). *Schulversuch 'Deutsch-Italienische Grundschule' Wolfsburg, gefördert aus Mitteln des Landes Niedersachsen und der EG-Kommission.* Dresden.

SANDFUCHS, U. (1996). Bilinguale Erziehung in der Grundschule. Das Beispiel der deutsch-italienischen Grundschule in Wolfsburg. *Wissenschaftliche Zeitschrift der Technischen Universität Dresden,* 45, 17–22.

SCHEERENS, J. (1992). *Effective schooling.* London: Cassell.

SEEBAUER, R. (1996). Frühes Fremdsprachenlernen. Einige Befunde zur Lautimitation und Lautdiskrimination im Kontext des Wiener Schulversuchs 'English auf der Grundstufe I'. *Erziehung und Unterricht,* 146 (2) 78–81.

SINGLETON, D. & LENGYEL, Z. (1995). *The age factor in second language acquisition.* Clevedon: Multilingual Matters .

SOLMECKE, G. (1997). Zur Dramaturgie des Deutschunterrichts: die Rolle der Steuerung. Beobachtungen im Deutschunterricht des Projekts 'Sprachbrücke'. In: LEGUTKE, M. *Unterrichtsforschung Fremdsprachenlernen Primarbereich.* (In Press).

SPADOLA, L. & TAESCHNER, T. (1991). Recitando s'impara in La scuola si aggiorna, 27–31, Nuova Eri – Edizioni Rai.

TAESCHNER, T. (1991). *A Developmental Psycholinguistic Approach to Second Language Teaching.* Ablex: Norwood.

TAESCHNER, T. (1993). *Insegnare con il format.* Roma: Anicia.

TEDDLIE, C. & SPRINGFIELD, S. (1993). *Schools make a difference: Lessons learned from a ten year study of school effects.* New York: Teachers College Press.

VINJÉ, M.P. (1993). *Balans van het Engels aan het einde van de basisschool.* Arnhem: CITO.

WODE H., BURMEISTER, P., DANIEL A., KICKLER, K.U. & KNUST, M. (1996). Die Erprobung von deutsch-englisch bilingualem Unterricht in Schleswig-Holstein: Ein erster Zwischenbericht. *Zeitschrift für Fremdsprachenforschung,* 7 (1) 15–42.

ZANGL, R. & PELTZER-KARPF, A. (1996). Vienna Bilingual Schooling: Die kurze Geschichte einer Langzeitstudie. *Unterrichtswissenschaft.*

The attached pages contain the framework developed by the group in order to process the various research projects.

The framework was originally developed in French, and the group is grateful to Paddy Carpenter for translating it into English.

# QUESTIONNAIRE

The aim is to collect together systematically information relating to experience accumulated in various Member States of the European Union ('experience' in the non-technical sense of the term, rather than a scientifically controlled experiment) in the teaching or learning of one or more foreign languages at primary or pre-primary level. The information should provide an answer to the following question:

*Under what conditions can one expect to obtain what sort of results?*

This presupposes the establishment of a relationship between the data received in the framework of the following terms:

The questionnaire set out below endeavours to discover this by grouping relevant elements under each of the two terms.

The questionnaire should be applied to publications (of various kinds such as reports, articles, etc.) describing experience in this field. It should help relevant information to be extrapolated in the framework described by the formula set out above.

The users of the questionnaire will be members of the expert group or any person engaged to help them with this task.

*Expert group on early language teaching*
Brussels, July 1996

---

1 Once again, the term has to be interpreted in its broadest sense, as will be shown by the various rubrics in the 'context' part of the following questionnaire.

**SUMMARY**

- Identification
- Intentions of the publication's author
- General characteristics of the project
- Stated objectives
- Language(s) concerned
- Place in the curriculum
- Learners
- Teachers
- Teaching methods
- Future plans of those in charge of the project
- Materials for the presentation of the project

**IDENTIFICATION**

| | |
|---|---|
| ➜ Country, town | ➜ |
| ➜ Name of the project | ➜ |
| ➜ Responsible individuals and institutions | ➜ |
| ➜ Source (publication which has been consulted) | ➜ |

**INTENTIONS OF THE PUBLICATION'S AUTHOR(S)**

State whether the author(s) has/have explicitly declared these intentions, or whether you have perceived them yourself.

| | |
|---|---|
| ➜ **Scope**<br><br>• isolated experiment with no possibility of generalising it in the short term<br>• isolated experiment with the possibility of generalising it in the short term<br>• part of a general teaching situation within the education system of a region or country | tick here |
| ➜ **Is it part of a research programme?**<br><br>• no<br>• yes (give the names of those responsible and the project's sponsors) | |
| ➜ **Degree of consensus**<br><br>• agreement with local authorities<br>• agreement with other teachers in the school<br>• agreement with parents | (1) |
| ➜ **Extra financial resources made available for the project**<br><br>• no<br>• yes (give details) | tick here |
| ➜ **Number of languages taught/presented to each pupil**<br><br>• *each pupil* learns/is exposed to *a single* language<br>• *each pupil* learns/is exposed to *several* languages<br>  state:<br>  • how many languages?<br>  • in what pattern? (e.g. three months per language) | |
| ➜ **If only one language is taught to each pupil, will the teaching of the language be continued in secondary education?**<br><br>• yes<br>• no | |

(1) Use one of the following symbols: Ø = none; – = not very much; ± = quite a lot; + = very well developed; * = total

**Quote the objectives given by the project promoters:**

→ objectives for the learner: (linguistic, educational, social etc.)

→ objectives for the education system: (e.g. to introduce a new language into the curriculum, to remove barriers between subjects etc.)

→

.

→ objectives for society:

→

**LANGUAGE(S) CONCERNED**

→ Which language(s) is/are taught (or presented) to the pupils?

→ If several languages are taught, what proportion of all pupils involved does each language represent?

→ In the case of each language, state whether it has a particular status for the pupils involved: e.g. the language is used in the local environment (e.g. regional language or near equivalent, migrant language or near equivalent), the language has a particular status (e.g. in the media etc.), the language of a neighbouring country (e.g. in border regions), the language has high status or the contrary etc.

| language | status |
|---|---|
| | |
| | |
| | |
| | |
| | |
| | |

CiLT

**PLACE IN THE CURRICULUM**

| Level | Age | Number of sessions per week | Length of the sessions | Number of hours per week | Number of hours per year |
|---|---|---|---|---|---|
| Pre-primary        -3 | | | | | |
| -2 | | | | | |
| -1 | | | | | |
| 1st year of primary | | | | | |
| 2nd year of primary | | | | | |
| 3rd year of primary | | | | | |
| 4th year of primary | | | | | |
| 5th year of primary | | | | | |
| 6th year of primary | | | | | |
| 7th year of primary | | | | | |

➜ Language teaching takes place?

- within the usual teaching timetable
- outside usual teaching hours

tick here

➜ Other remarks concerning the timetable:

→ **Total number of learners concerned** (or percentage of the total school population    →
of the country at the school level under consideration)

→ **Types of learners**

- is the group representative of the whole school population at a national or regional level according to the following dimensions?

| dimension | representative yes    no | if you have ticked 'no': state here the difference according to the whole school population[1] |
|---|---|---|
| • geographical position | | |
| • social origin | | |
| • type of school | | |
| • contacts with the language(s) concerned, the countries where it/they are spoken | | |
| • bilingual (mother tongue different to the one used in the school and to the one(s) being taught) | | |
| • general aptitudes, knowledge and general ability | | |
| • attitudes (their own or those of their parents) towards the language(s) | | |
| • attitudes towards learning | | |
| • ethnic group, gender etc. | | |

- Have these differences been assessed in a rigorous fashion?
  If so, by what process?

(1) Where it appears necessary, for each answer, state for what proportion of all the pupils concerned this does apply.

➡ **Status** nothing said about the teacher                                                   tick

- primary or pre-primary trained                                                              **x**

  - to teach all subjects
  - to teach certain subjects only (other than foreign languages)
    which subjects?
  - trained only to teach foreign languages

  - which subjects do they teach in the classes concerned?
    - only foreign languages
    - languages and other subjects
      which subjects?

- language specialists trained to teach in secondary education

- 'visiting teachers' (e.g. native speaker without teacher training)

- others (give details)

➡ **Teacher training specific to language teaching at this level**

| field of training | initial | in-service | length | description |
|---|---|---|---|---|
| • general grasp of language | | | | |
| • grasp of the specific language for the fields targeted | | | | |
| • primary or pre-primary teaching | | | | |
| • general principles of foreign language teaching | | | | |
| • teaching languages at primary or pre-primary level | | | | |
| • others (give details) | | | | |

(1) Where it appears necessary, for each answer, state for what proportion of all the pupils concerned this does apply.

➔ **Linguistic knowledge and ability — NOT MENTIONED**      tick

- for the language to be taught

  - ability to communicate
    - mother tongue
    - near native speaker
    - good
    - limited
    - very weak

  - metalinguistic knowledge
    - highly developed
    - fairly well developed
    - almost non-existent

- for the language used at the school

  - ability to communicate
    - mother tongue
    - near native speaker
    - good
    - limited
    - very weak

  - metalinguistic knowledge
    - highly developed
    - fairly well developed
    - almost non-existent

➔ **Cultural knowledge and ability**

- for the culture(s) of the language(s) to be taught

    - originated from this culture
    - good
    - quite good
    - limited
    - very weak

- for the comparison between cultures

    - good
    - fairly good
    - limited
    - very weak

- for the European dimension

    - good
    - fairly good
    - limited
    - very weak

## TEACHERS (CONTINUED)

| → Attitudes towards the project | tick | why |
|---|---|---|
| • very positive<br>• fairly positive<br>• fairly negative<br>• very negative | | |

| → Isolation | tick |
|---|---|
| • the teachers are isolated<br>• the teachers work in a network | |

## TEACHING METHODS

| → Activities | Ø | − | ± | + | * |
|---|---|---|---|---|---|
| • oral<br>• written | | | | | |
| **→ Activities**<br>• comprehension<br>• expression<br>  • repetition<br>  • production | | | | | |
| **→ Types of activity**<br>• stories (invented and dramatised)<br>• dialogues, sketches<br>• interrupted sentences (let's make the word..., 2nd year)<br>• games (competitions etc. mimicry, treasure hunt)<br>• role playing<br>• learning by doing (drawings)<br>• observing the foreign language<br>• comparing the mother tongue with the foreign language | | | | | |
| **→ How the activities are conducted**<br>• individual activities<br>• in small groups<br>• by whole class | | | | | |

| → Use of aids | Give details | Ø | − | ± | + | * |
|---|---|---|---|---|---|---|
| • written<br>• aural<br>• using symbols<br>• audio-visual<br>• computer-assisted (text only)<br>• multimedia (computer assisted)<br>• others (e.g. puppets) | | | | | | |

| | Ø | – | ± | + | * |
|---|---|---|---|---|---|
| ➜ **Teaching materials**<br>• use of a complete commercial package<br>• use of various materials chosen by the teacher<br>• use of materials made by the teacher | | | | | |
| ➜ **Introduction of cultural elements**<br>• concerning the foreign culture(s)<br>• comparison between cultures<br>• the European dimension | | | | | |
| ➜ Introduction of the foreign language into class activities (i.e. no time specifically set aside for the foreign language). Give details: | | | | | |
| ➜ Is teaching carried out exclusively in the foreign language during activities devoted to teaching it? *I suppose*<br>no **x**    yes ❑<br><br>• if you have ticked 'no', please state what relative share is given to each language<br>  • mother tongue (for talking in general)<br>  • foreign language (for the specific topics)<br><br>• What part do non-verbal methods play in communications between teacher and pupils? | | | | | |
| ➜ Exchanges with pupils whose mother tongue is the target language (give details) | | | | | |
| ➜ The teaching method has been defined according to a specific theoretical approach. Give details: not mentioned | | | | | |
| ➜ The teaching method is in keeping with current thinking. In the case that this is not so, please explain:<br>It does take into account usual thinking in L2 teaching to older children or adolescents; it does not use up dated methodology for children. | | | | | |
| ➜ (Average) number of pupils per class (or section) | ➜ | | | | |

(1) Use one of the following symbols: Ø = non-existent; – = not well developed; ± = quite well developed;
+ = very well developed; & = omnipresent (or exclusive)

C*i*LT

## FUTURE PLANS OF THOSE IN CHARGE OF THE PROJECT

What initiatives do those in charge of the project plan (or have they planned) to take *following* the completion of the project described?

➡

➡    Research initiatives:

## MATERIALS FOR THE PRESENTATION OF THE PROJECT

Are there other presentation materials for the project (video of classroom activities, teaching materials etc.)? If so, please give references.

**On the status of languages (not presented in the project)**

To be used only if you have ticked R+ in one of the tables in Part B.

> What in your opinion is the quality of the methodology used in this research?
> What are its weak and strong points?